LISTENING PRACTICE FOR ELEMENTARY STUDENTS

# Listen carefully

D0508022

INSTITUTE FOR APPLIED LANGUAGE STUDIES
**UNIVERSITY OF EDINBURGH**
21 Hill Place
Edinburgh EH8 9DP

JACK C. RICHARDS

Oxford University Press
Walton Street, Oxford OX2 6DP

Oxford  New York  Toronto
Petaling Jaya  Singapore  Hong Kong  Tokyo
Delhi  Bombay  Calcutta  Madras  Karachi
Nairobi  Dar es Salaam  Cape Town
Melbourne  Auckland

*and associated companies in*
Berlin  Ibadan

*Oxford* and *Oxford English* are trade
marks of Oxford University Press

ISBN 0 19 457280 3
© Oxford University Press 1990

First published 1990
Second impression 1991

All rights reserved. No part of this publication may be
reproduced, stored in a retrieval system, or transmitted,
in any form or by any means, electronic, mechanical,
photocopying, recording or otherwise, without the
prior permission of Oxford University Press.

This book is sold subject to the condition that it shall
not, by way of trade or otherwise, be lent, re-sold, hired
out or otherwise circulated without the publisher's
prior consent in any form of binding or cover other
than that in which it is published and without a similar
condition being imposed on the subseqent purchaser.

The publishers would like to thank the following for
their assistance and permission to reproduce
photographs:

The Ashmolean Museum
The Austrian National Tourist Office
J Allan Cash
British Airways
Mary Evans
Ford Motor Company Ltd
Honda UK
Mansell Collection
Renault UK Ltd
Popperfoto
Volvo Trucks (Great Britain) Ltd
Philip Warren (Taxis)

Illustrations by:

Kevin Baverstock
Roy Ingram
Damon Burnard
Oxford Illustrators
John Montgomery
Steve Jenkins
Mike Nicholson
Paul Richardson

Set in Palatino

Printed in Hong Kong

**CONTENTS**

## INTRODUCTION

## UNIT 1
### Numbers

### Telephone numbers

### Addresses

## UNIT 2
### Names

### Meeting people

### Places

## UNIT 3
### Times

### Dates

## UNIT 4
### Food

### Recipes

### In a restaurant

## UNIT 5
### Furniture and rooms

### At home

## UNIT 6
### Prices

# CONTENTS

# UNIT 13

## Leisure activities

## Invitations and arrangements

# UNIT 14

## Instructions

# UNIT 15

## Airports

## Immigration

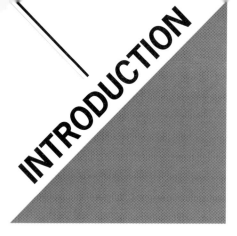

## INTRODUCTION TO THE TEACHER

*Listen carefully* is a book of listening practice activities for adult and young adult students of English at elementary level. It can be used either in the classroom with guidance from the teacher or as a self-study book for the student working alone. It is also suitable for use in a language laboratory.

The recorded material is provided on two C90 cassettes. It contains a variety of voices and British accents. Some of the situational dialogues involve foreign visitors to Britain and contain American, Australian and non-native speakers. The timing of each activity is given in the transcript (pp62-84).

*Listen carefully* contains fifteen topic-based units which cover a wide variety of everyday situations. Within each unit activities are grouped into sections around one aspect of the topic. Material can easily be selected for practice with reference to the Contents (ppi-iii). We strongly advise teachers to work through complete sections of a unit in order for the sequencing of exercise types to be effective. The key and transcript are given at the back of the book.

### Grading

Thorough and systematic practice of the micro-skills of listening are given by means of grading the activities in each section. In grading the activities three main factors have been taken into consideration. The first is the complexity of the language input. At the beginning of a unit students are only exposed to explicit language; the amount of redundant language and inferential work necessary for comprehension is increased gradually. The second factor is the context of the listening activity. All the topics covered should be familiar to the students. This will enable them to identify with the situation, bring in their own knowledge and experience of it and to have expectations based on this experience. Thirdly, students are guided through a sequence of exercises as follows (where relevant to the topic or situation):

- ▶ distinguishing a particular sound or similar-sounding word in isolation
- ▶ recognizing a particular sound or word in speech
- ▶ clarifying information
- ▶ calculating something on the basis of information heard
- ▶ recognizing attitudes and opinions
- ▶ inferring meaning
- ▶ being in the position of participant in a dialogue and choosing the best response.

Where possible the opening activity of a unit or section gives practice in pronunciation and word stress.

Note that activities marked * are not on the tape.

### Pre-listening

Whether or not the topic area chosen is the same as other recent classwork, it is important to spend some time setting the scene for each group of activities. You may want to ask students to recall work from their coursebook on this topic or perhaps take in some pictures or other prompts to use as a starting point for a brief class discussion. Encourage students to talk about their knowledge and experience of the subject. Elicit as much relevant language as possible. Before the lesson read through the tapescript. Pre-teach any new words and phrases in class. Some of the opening activities combine vocabulary work and pronunciation. Let students work on their own when classifying vocabulary, comparing their answers in pairs. Where pronunciation is the focus, it is advisable to go through the activity with the whole class first, letting students practise on their own when you feel they are ready. The pronunciation activities are recorded on the tape.

### Procedure

1 The different types of activity are listed above. For all activities it is very important for students to know exactly what they have to listen for, and how they are expected to complete the task. Go through the instructions with them. Make sure they are familiar with using a tick to show that something is correct and a cross to show that something is wrong. Boxes or lines are provided for this. Students may be asked to circle the answer, or to add numbers next to items. Sometimes they will be required to write words or phrases in tables.

2 Where the activity is based on short dialogues or is a continuous text, students should listen to it once through with their books closed to get a general idea of the situation. Play the tape as many times as necessary for students to complete the exercise. There is no need for them to be put under any time pressure. Stop the tape after a few questions or a short section to give students time to work out their answers.

3 When they have completed an activity students discuss their answers in pairs or small groups. Then go through the answers with the whole class playing the tape, stopping at key information points to confirm the correct answers.

4 It is important to remember that the material in *Listen carefully* is for practice, not testing. If students have had difficulty completing a particular activity they can try it again before going on to the next one.

## INTRODUCTION TO THE STUDENT

*Listen carefully* helps you to practise listening to English and to understand what you hear. Two C90 cassettes go with this book. There are 15 units on everyday topics like food, shopping and holidays. You can do the units in any order but the ones at the beginning of the book are easier than the units at the end.

### How to use *Listen carefully*

1 Look at the Contents (pages i-iii) and choose a whole unit or section of a unit you want to practise. For example, Furniture and rooms, from Unit 5. If you choose a section of a unit do all the activities in order.

2 Read the instructions carefully. It is very important for you to understand what you must listen for.

3 Find the correct place on the tape. Activities marked * are not on the tape.

4 There are different ways of answering an activity.

Tick the correct address.

☑ 89 Mount Street

Circle the numbers you hear.

12        20        ⟨22⟩

Number the names you hear from 1 - 8.
Short

Write down the arrival time using the twenty-four hour clock.    07.45

5 For each activity play the tape through once without writing anything. Get a general understanding of the situation. Play the tape as many times as you need to answer the questions. You may want to stop it several times to think about what you have heard and to write down your answers.

6 Remember, you do not have to understand every word on the tape to complete the activity.

7 When you finish writing your answers, listen to the tape through again to check them. Then turn to the Key (pages 62-84) and mark your work.

8 If you found an exercise difficult, do it again. Sometimes it will help to read the transcript (pages 85-94) but do not do this when you are doing an activity for the first time.

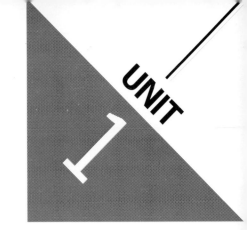

# Numbers

## Activity 1

Say these numbers out loud.

5   17   27   89   7   30   39   51   80

120   349   409   411   579   614   732   925

1,003   1,012   1,120   1,376   1,539   1,630   1,780   1,899   1,905

Now listen to the tape and check that you said them correctly.

## Activity 2

Listen to the tape. You will hear seven numbers. Circle the numbers you hear.

| | | | |
|---|---|---|---|
| 1 | 12 | 20 | (22) |
| 2 | 109 | 119 | 190 |
| 3 | 33 | 13 | 30 |
| 4 | 1001 | 1010 | 1100 |
| 5 | 70 | 7 | 17 |
| 6 | 150 | 115 | 151 |
| 7 | 1509 | 1559 | 1590 |

## Activity 3

Listen to the prizes in a lottery. What were the winning numbers? Circle the correct number for each prize.

| | | | |
|---|---|---|---|
| Seventh prize | 151 | 150 | (115) |
| Sixth prize | 1707 | 1770 | 1777 |
| Fifth prize | 91 | 19 | 90 |
| Fourth prize | 390 | 309 | 319 |
| Third prize | 55 | 53 | 59 |
| Second prize | 1990 | 1999 | 1099 |
| First prize | 14 | 40 | 44 |

# Telephone numbers

## Activity 1

Read these telephone numbers out loud.

0830 941557     01 308 3378     0274 38826     051 43 378
061 352 2899     86 451283     021 616 7425     0462 623728

Now listen to the tape and check that you said them correctly.

## Activity 2

You will hear nine telephone numbers. Tick the numbers you hear.

| 1 | ☐ 313557 | 4 | ☐ 0509 23092 | 7 | ☐ 058 90 789 |
| | ✓ 313597 | | ☐ 0519 23092 | | ☐ 068 91 789 |
| 2 | ☐ 743678 | 5 | ☐ 0457 64332 | 8 | ☐ 335278 |
| | ☐ 743670 | | ☐ 0457 64323 | | ☐ 335279 |
| 3 | ☐ 01 800 7689 | 6 | ☐ 041 914 5389 | | ☐ 339279 |
| | ☐ 01 808 7680 | | ☐ 041 904 5308 | 9 | ☐ 0425 5781 |
| | ☐ 01 808 7688 | | ☐ 041 940 5388 | | ☐ 0425 5718 |

## Activity 3*

Write down the first name of each person in your class. Each person says his or her telephone number. Wait a few seconds, then see if you can still remember the number and write it down. Check the numbers with your partner.

## Activity 4

Listen to people asking Directory Enquiries for telephone numbers for the places below. Write down the correct numbers.

John Radcliffe Hospital .... *Oxford 64711* ....................

Odeon Cinema ................................................

Shangri-la Restaurant ........................................

London University ...........................................

County Hall .................................................

British Airways .............................................

## Activity 5

Listen to people telephoning the places below. Did they dial the right number or not? Tick the correct box, right or wrong.

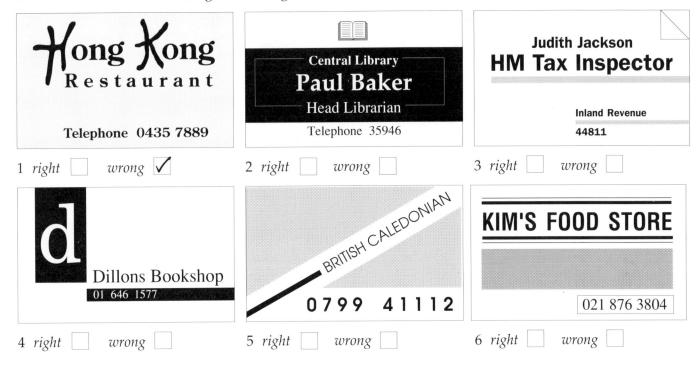

# Hong Kong
### Restaurant

**Telephone 0435 7889**

1 *right* ☐ *wrong* ✓

---

**Central Library**
## Paul Baker
Head Librarian

Telephone 35946

2 *right* ☐ *wrong* ☐

---

**Judith Jackson**
# HM Tax Inspector

**Inland Revenue**
**44811**

3 *right* ☐ *wrong* ☐

---

## d Dillons Bookshop
**01 646 1577**

4 *right* ☐ *wrong* ☐

---

*BRITISH CALEDONIAN*

**0799 41112**

5 *right* ☐ *wrong* ☐

---

## KIM'S FOOD STORE

021 876 3804

6 *right* ☐ *wrong* ☐

# Addresses

## Activity 1

Listen to people asking for the addresses of these places. Tick the correct address.

1  American Express
☐ 890 Mount Street
☐ 819 Mount Street
✓ 89 Mount Street

2  Asia Pacific Travel
☐ 123 Waterloo Road
☐ 103 Waterloo Road
☐ 13 Waterloo Road

3  Black and Decker
☐ 603 Holloway Road
☐ 623 Hollow Way
☐ 623 Holloway Road

4  Gulf House
☐ 2 Portman Square, W1
☐ 2 Portman Street, W1
☐ 2 Portman Street, W11

5  Pan American
☐ 193 Piccadilly
☐ 153 Piccadilly
☐ 139 Piccadilly

6  Eastman Dental Hospital
☐ 256 Grayson Road
☐ 265 Grays Inn Road
☐ 256 Grays Inn Road

### Activity 2

Listen to people giving their addresses. Complete the missing information.

1  .. *313* .... Cumberland Avenue.

2  ............ University Drive, flat .......... .

3  ............ Wellington Street.

4  ............ Grant Street.

5  ............ Judd Street, flat .......... .

# Names

## Activity 1

First listen to the tape. Then say these surnames out loud.

| | | | | |
|---|---|---|---|---|
| George | Jones | Richards | Simpson | Thomson |
| Gordon | Johnson | Richmond | Samson | Thomas |
| Gray | Harris | Short | Schmidt | Winters |
| Graham | Harrison | Shaw | Smith | Wilson |

## Activity 2

Some of the people from Activity 1 will give their names. Number the names you hear from 1 - 8.

## Activity 3*

How do you spell these people's first names?

1 .....Eddie.....................  2 ..............................  3 ..............................

4 .............................  5 .............................  6 .............................

5

### Activity 4*

Ask your partner what his/her father's first name and surname are and write them down.

### Activity 5

Listen to people opening bank accounts. Write down their names.

| *first name* | *surname* |
|---|---|
| 1. Tosh | Asada |
| 2. | |
| 3. | |
| 4. | |
| 5. | |
| 6. | |
| 7. | |
| 8. | |

### Activity 6

Listen. Did the bank clerk write down these people's names correctly? Put a tick beside the names if they are spelled correctly. Correct the names with the wrong spelling.

| | | |
|---|---|---|
| 1. Jesse Bowman | ☐ | Jessie Bowman |
| 2. Trisha Everette | ☐ | |
| 3. Seichi Shimamoto | ☐ | |
| 4. Karla Mestenza | ☐ | |
| 5. Dorothy Hazzard | ☐ | |
| 6. Fernando Gomez | ☐ | |
| 7. Ronald Cohen | ☐ | |
| 8. Bradley Metcalf | ☐ | |

## Activity 7

What are these people's titles (e.g. Ms, Mrs, Miss, Mr, or Dr) and initials (e.g. J C )? Listen and complete the guest register for a hotel.

**TOWER HOTEL**

| Name | Home Addre |
|------|------------|
| Aqrabanti | |
| Foster | |
| Corpuz | |
| Kato | |
| Blackburn | |
| Chun | |
| Lange | |
| Corrigan | |

# Meeting people

## Activity 1

Work in pairs. A reads out each greeting and B gives a reply. Take it in turns to be A and B. Then listen to some examples on the tape and write them down.

1   Good morning. How are you today? ........ *Fine, thanks.* ........................

2   Nice day, isn't it? ...............................................................

3   How was your weekend? ...........................................................

4   Hi. How's everything? ............................................................

5   Hello. My name's Pat. ...........................................................

6   What did you say your name was? .................................................

7   Nice to meet you. ...............................................................

8   How do you do? ..................................................................

9   How're you doing? ...............................................................

10   See you later. .................................................................

11   Have a nice day. ...............................................................

### Activity 2

Listen and tick the best reply to each sentence.

1  ☐ Yes, please.
   ☑ That's right.
   ☐ No, thanks.

4  ☐ How do you do?
   ☐ Yes, I do.
   ☐ That's right.

2  ☐ Yes, I have.
   ☐ To the bank.
   ☐ Fine, thanks.

5  ☐ Yes, it is.
   ☐ Yes, thanks.
   ☐ Fine, thanks.

3  ☐ You're welcome.
   ☐ Nice to meet you, too.
   ☐ How do you do?

6  ☐ Nice to meet you.
   ☐ Have a nice day.
   ☐ Is it?

# Places

## Activity 1

You will hear the names of some British counties. Tick the counties you hear.

1  ☑ Berkshire
   ☐ Buckinghamshire

5  ☐ Lincolnshire
   ☐ Leicestershire
   ☐ Lancashire

2  ☐ Cambridgeshire
   ☐ Cornwall

6  ☐ Merseyside
   ☐ Tayside

3  ☐ Devon
   ☐ Durham
   ☐ Dorset

7  ☐ Strathclyde
   ☐ Staffordshire

4  ☐ Gwent
   ☐ Kent

8  ☐ West Glamorgan
   ☐ West Midlands

## Activity 2

These people are American. Where are they from? Listen and tick the correct state.

1 Pueblo
   ☐ Kansas
   ☑ Colorado
   ☐ Utah

5 Harrisburg
   ☐ West Virginia
   ☐ Indiana
   ☐ Pennsylvania

2 Wayne
   ☐ Ohio
   ☐ Illinois
   ☐ Indiana

6 Prescott
   ☐ Arizona
   ☐ New Mexico
   ☐ California

3 Springfield
   ☐ Illinois
   ☐ Indiana
   ☐ Iowa

7 Great Falls
   ☐ North Dakota
   ☐ Montana
   ☐ Wyoming

4 Birmingham
   ☐ Georgia
   ☐ Alabama
   ☐ Mississippi

8 Salem
   ☐ Oregon
   ☐ Washington
   ☐ Idaho

## Activity 3

Where are these people living now? Listen and tick the correct city or country.

1 ☐ London
   ☑ Manchester

2 ☐ Paris
   ☐ New York

3 ☐ Tokyo
   ☐ Hong Kong

4 ☐ Dallas
   ☐ St Louis

5 ☐ Barcelona
   ☐ Madrid

6 ☐ Italy
   ☐ France

7 ☐ Mexico
   ☐ Ecuador

8 ☐ Cambridge
   ☐ Oxford

## Activity 4

Listen to the students in a class introduce themselves. How many students come from each of the areas below?

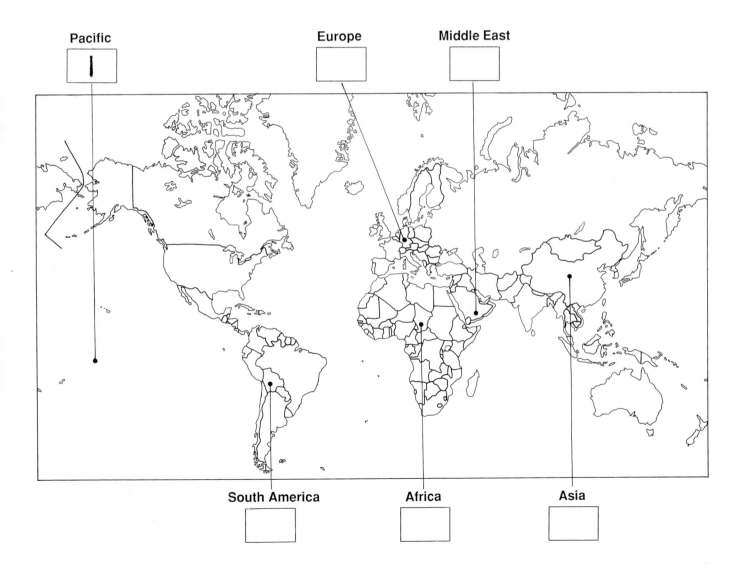

# Times

## Activity 1

Look at the watches below and say the times. Then listen to the tape and check that you said them correctly.

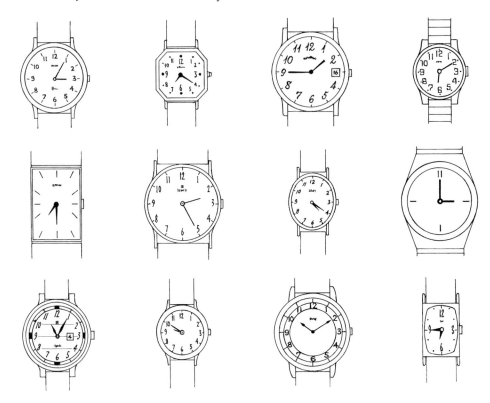

## Activity 2*

Work in pairs. Student A reads one of the times shown below. Student B circles the time he/she hears. Take it in turns to be A and B.

| | | | |
|---|---|---|---|
| 1 | 3.13 | 3.30 | 3.03 |
| 2 | 9.40 | 9.20 | 9.14 |
| 3 | 12.05 | 12.15 | 12.50 |
| 4 | 1.55 | 1.05 | 1.15 |
| 5 | 3.14 | 3.40 | 3.44 |
| 6 | 7.10 | 10.07 | 7.07 |
| 7 | 4.15 | 4.50 | 4.55 |
| 8 | 6.30 | 6.35 | 6.25 |

## Activity 3

Listen to people asking when the flights below arrive. Write down the arrival times using the twenty-four hour clock.

| Flight no. | Arrival time | Flight no. | Arrival time |
|---|---|---|---|
| 1 TW218 | 7.45 | 5 A115 | |
| 2 BA13 | | 6 AF35 | |
| 3 AF409 | | 7 SK70 | |
| 4 LH68 | | 8 BA502 | |

## Activity 4

Listen to people telephoning an office to speak to the people below. Write down the time when each person will return. It is now 10 a.m. If the operator says, 'He'll be back in an hour.' write 11.00.

| | Returning at | | Returning at |
|---|---|---|---|
| Mr Day | ..11:00.. | Mrs Ginatti | . . . . . . . . . . |
| Ms Lewis | . . . . . . . . . . | Mr Frank | . . . . . . . . . . |
| Mr Grant | . . . . . . . . . . | Ms Taylor | . . . . . . . . . . |

## Activity 5

Listen to people calling the international telephone operator to ask about the time in the countries below. The caller's time is shown. Listen and write down the time in the country they ask about. For example, if the caller's time is 2 p.m. and the time in Bolivia is four hours behind, the time there is 10 a.m.

*Caller's time*

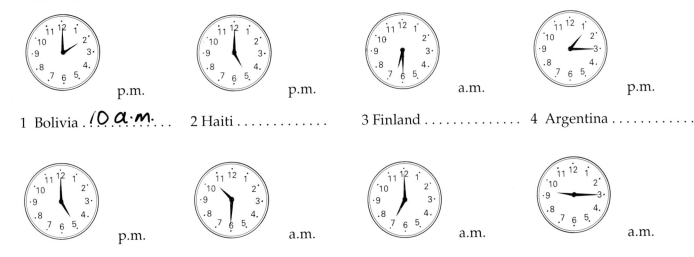

1 Bolivia ..10 a.m...    2 Haiti . . . . . . . . . . .     3 Finland . . . . . . . . . . . . .    4 Argentina . . . . . . . . . . .

5 Burma . . . . . . . . . . . . . 6 Taiwan . . . . . . . . . .     7 Fiji . . . . . . . . . . .      8 Germany . . . . . . . . . . .

# Dates

## Activity 1

Say these years out loud. Now listen to the tape and check that you said them correctly.

| | | | | | | |
|---|---|---|---|---|---|---|
| 1879 | 1952 | 1539 | 1800 | 1978 | 1760 | 1913 |
| 1817 | 1901 | 1970 | 1929 | 1899 | 1908 | 1066 |

## Activity 2

When did these famous writers live? Listen and write down when they were born and when they died.

1 Charles Dickens

born 1812 died 1870

2 D H Lawrence

born ........ died ........

3 Jane Austen

born ........ died ........

4 Ernest Hemingway

born ........ died ........

5 Emily Dickinson

born ........ died ........

6 Oscar Wilde

born ........ died ........

## Activity 3

Say these dates out loud. Then listen to the tape and check that you said them correctly.

| | | | | |
|---|---|---|---|---|
| 7/6/48 | 8/2/85 | 23/3/80 | 2/1/84 | 14/11/87 |
| 24/12/62 | 4/9/72 | 3/10/21 | 8/7/56 | 29/2/80 |

## Activity 4

Listen to these people saying when they were born. Write down the dates. For example, if you hear, 'I was born on the 28th of July, 1953.' write 28/7/53.

1 .....6/6/39.....    4 ........................

2 ........................    5 ........................

3 ........................    6 ........................

## Activity 5

When did these visitors arrive in Britain and when will they leave? Listen and circle the day each person arrived and the day they are leaving.

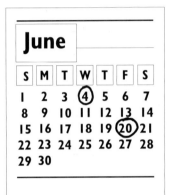

**June**

| S | M | T | W | T | F | S |
|---|---|---|---|---|---|---|
| 1 | 2 | 3 | ④ | 5 | 6 | 7 |
| 8 | 9 | 10 | 11 | 12 | 13 | 14 |
| 15 | 16 | 17 | 18 | 19 | ⑳ | 21 |
| 22 | 23 | 24 | 25 | 26 | 27 | 28 |
| 29 | 30 | | | | | |

1

**JUNE**

| Sun | 1 | 8 | 15 | 22 | 29 |
|---|---|---|---|---|---|
| Mon | 2 | 9 | 16 | 23 | 30 |
| Tue | 3 | 10 | 17 | 24 | |
| Wed | 4 | 11 | 18 | 25 | |
| Thu | 5 | 12 | 19 | 26 | |
| Fri | 6 | 13 | 20 | 27 | |
| Sat | 7 | 14 | 21 | 28 | |

2

**JUNE**

| S | M | T | W | T | F | S |
|---|---|---|---|---|---|---|
| 1 | 2 | 3 | 4 | 5 | 6 | 7 |
| 8 | 9 | 10 | 11 | 12 | 13 | 14 |
| 15 | 16 | 17 | 18 | 19 | 20 | 21 |
| 22 | 23 | 24 | 25 | 26 | 27 | 28 |
| 29 | 30 | | | | | |

3

**J U N E**

| S | 1 | 8 | 15 | 22 | 29 |
|---|---|---|---|---|---|
| M | 2 | 9 | 16 | 23 | 30 |
| T | 3 | 10 | 17 | 24 | |
| W | 4 | 11 | 18 | 25 | |
| T | 5 | 12 | 19 | 26 | |
| F | 6 | 13 | 20 | 27 | |
| S | 7 | 14 | 21 | 28 | |

4

**JUNE**

| S | M | T | W | T | F | S |
|---|---|---|---|---|---|---|
| 1 | 2 | 3 | 4 | 5 | 6 | 7 |
| 8 | 9 | 10 | 11 | 12 | 13 | 14 |
| 15 | 16 | 17 | 18 | 19 | 20 | 21 |
| 22 | 23 | 24 | 25 | 26 | 27 | 28 |
| 29 | 30 | | | | | |

5

**JUNE**

| S | M | T | W | T | F | S |
|---|---|---|---|---|---|---|
| 1 | 2 | 3 | 4 | 5 | 6 | 7 |
| 8 | 9 | 10 | 11 | 12 | 13 | 14 |
| 15 | 16 | 17 | 18 | 19 | 20 | 21 |
| 22 | 23 | 24 | 25 | 26 | 27 | 28 |
| 29 | 30 | | | | | |

6

## Activity 6

How long have these people been in Britain? Listen and write the number of weeks, months, or years they have been here.

1 .....6½ weeks.....    5 ........................

2 ........................    6 ........................

3 ........................    7 ........................

4 ........................    8 ........................

# Food

## Activity 1

Put these words into the table under the correct headings.

| mango | beef | chicken | grapefruit | wheat |
| tuna | salmon | apple | broccoli | rice |
| sole | turkey | orange | corn | pear |
| cucumber | onion | lobster | lamb | |
| pineapple | cabbage | mushroom | cauliflower | |

*mango* is underlined.

| *meat* | *fish* | *vegetables* | *fruit* | *cereals* |
|--------|--------|--------------|---------|-----------|
|        |        |              | mango   |           |

Now listen to how some of the words are pronounced and underline the stressed syllable, for example, <u>man</u>go.

## Activity 2

You will hear sentences containing the phrase 'a' or 'the'. Listen and tick the one you hear.

| | | |
|---|---|---|
| 1 | ☐ a cauliflower | ✓ the cauliflower |
| 2 | ☐ a grapefruit | ☐ the grapefruit |
| 3 | ☐ a cabbage | ☐ the cabbage |
| 4 | ☐ a salmon | ☐ the salmon |
| 5 | ☐ a lobster | ☐ the lobster |
| 6 | ☐ a pineapple | ☐ the pineapple |
| 7 | ☐ a cucumber | ☐ the cucumber |

## Activity 3

Tim is going to the supermarket. Listen and tick the things he needs to buy.

| | |
|---|---|
| ☐ cucumber | ☐ cabbage |
| ☐ bread | ☐ onions |
| ☐ sweetcorn | ✓ broccoli |
| ☐ lamb | ☐ rice |

# Recipes

## Activity 1

You will hear the ingredients for three recipes. Listen and write down the amounts needed. Use these abbreviations:

g = grams
kg = kilograms
l = litre(s)
tsp = teaspoon(s)
tbsp = tablespoon(s)

**1**
800g beef
onions
tomato purée
curry powder
salt
pepper

**2**
eggs
onions
mushrooms
cream
salt
pepper
cheese

**3**
chicken
onions
chopped bacon
red wine
flour

# In a restaurant

## Activity 1

You will hear a waiter taking people's orders in a restaurant. Listen and tick their orders.

**1**

Menu

| | Price |
|---|---|
| ☐ **Beef** | |
| well done | |
| medium | |
| rare | |
| ✓ **chicken** | |
| ☐ **fish** | |
| ☐ **rice** | |
| ☐ **potatoes** | |
| ☐ **vegetables** | |
| ☐ **tea** | |
| ☐ **coffee** | |
| ☐ **fruit juice** | Total |

**2**

Menu

| | Price |
|---|---|
| ☐ **Beef** | |
| well done | |
| medium | |
| rare | |
| ☐ **chicken** | |
| ☐ **fish** | |
| ☐ **rice** | |
| ☐ **potatoes** | |
| ☐ **vegetables** | |
| ☐ **tea** | |
| ☐ **coffee** | |
| ☐ **fruit juice** | |
| | Total |

**3**

Menu

| | Price |
|---|---|
| ☐ **Beef** | |
| well done | |
| medium | |
| rare | |
| ☐ **chicken** | |
| ☐ **fish** | |
| ☐ **rice** | |
| ☐ **potatoes** | |
| ☐ **vegetables** | |
| ☐ **tea** | |
| ☐ **coffee** | |
| ☐ **fruit juice** | |
| | Total |

## Activity 2

Listen to people talking about their meals. Did they enjoy their food? Tick the correct response for each speaker.

|   | *Yes, they liked it a lot.* | *Yes, they quite liked it.* | *No, they didn't like it at all.* |
|---|---|---|---|
| 1 | ✓ | | |
| 2 | | | |
| 3 | | | |
| 4 | | | |
| 5 | | | |
| 6 | | | |

## Activity 3

Listen to people talking about their food. What do they mean? Tick the correct explanation.

1 ....... too hot ..✓.... not hot enough

2 ....... undercooked ....... overcooked

3 ....... too salty ....... not salty enough

4 ....... too tough ....... too salty

5 ....... undercooked ....... overcooked

6 ....... too spicy ....... not spicy enough

7 ....... too much sugar ....... not enough sugar

## Activity 4

Listen to the waitress and choose the best response.

1 ✓ Yes, it's fine. / Yes, please.

2 ☐ Yes, it is. / Fine, thanks.

3 ☐ No, thanks. / Not at all.

4 ☐ No, thanks. / Yes, it is.

5 ☐ Yes, I do. / Just a little.

6 ☐ Yes, please. / Yes, it's great.

7 ☐ Not just now. / No, it isn't.

# Furniture and rooms

## Activity 1*

In which rooms of a house do we usually find the things below? Put them into the correct rooms in the table.

a wardrobe          a television

a sofa              a sink

a wash basin        a stereo system

a cooker            a shower

a chest of drawers  a reading lamp

a fireplace         a washing machine

a fridge            a bookcase

| *the kitchen* | *the living room* | *the bathroom* | *a bedroom* |
|---|---|---|---|
| | | | *a wardrobe* |

## Activity 2

You will hear eight of the words from the list above. Number the words you hear from 1 - 8, and underline the stressed syllable, for example, <u>war</u>drobe.

## Activity 3

Rita wants to rent a flat. You will hear her talking to a landlord about it. Which room is the landlord describing? Tick a or b.

1a ✓ b ☐

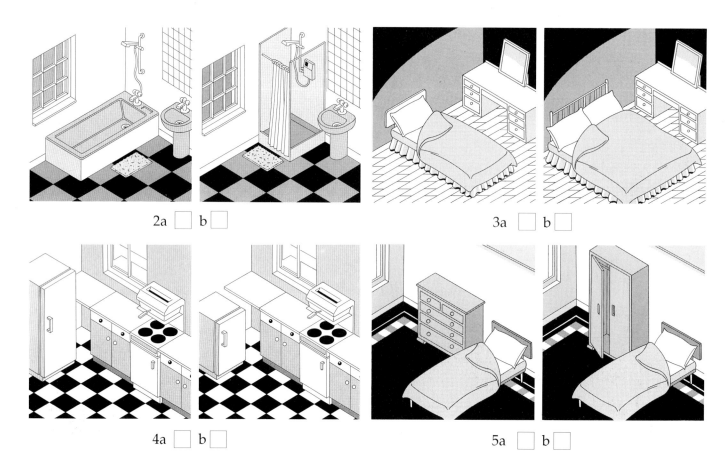

2a ☐ b ☐

3a ☐ b ☐

4a ☐ b ☐

5a ☐ b ☐

## Activity 4

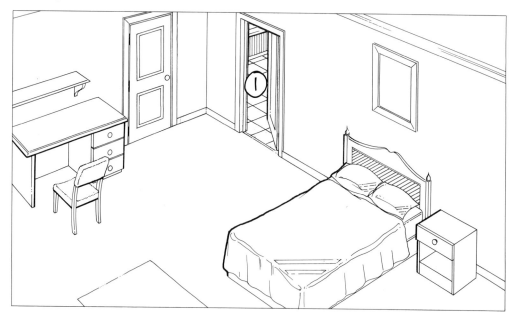

Mrs Keane has just arrived at her hotel. Listen to the porter showing her where things are in her room. Number the correct places in the picture.

1 towels
2 light switch for the bathroom
3 phone
4 phone book

5 kettle
6 information about the hotel
7 ashtray

## Activity 5

Listen to people talking about where they live. Tick the picture of the house or building they are talking about.

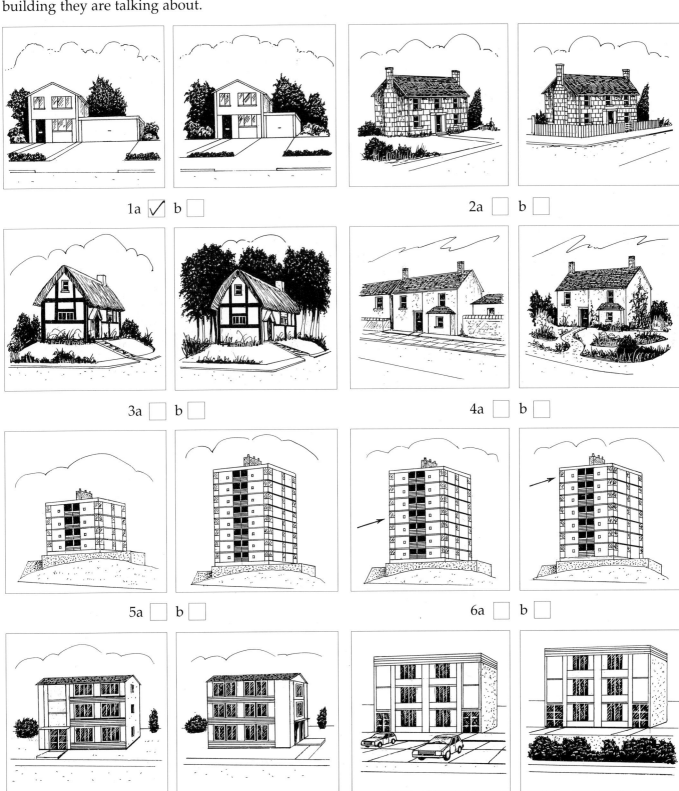

1a ✓   b ☐                          2a ☐   b ☐

3a ☐   b ☐                          4a ☐   b ☐

5a ☐   b ☐                          6a ☐   b ☐

7a ☐   b ☐                          8a ☐   b ☐

# At home

### Activity 1

Listen to people phoning their friends. Tick where each person is.

|  | Kathy | Bill | Susan | Terry | Mr Lee | Helen |
|---|---|---|---|---|---|---|
| in the garage | ✓ |  |  |  |  |  |
| in the bathroom |  |  |  |  |  |  |
| in the bedroom |  |  |  |  |  |  |
| in the kitchen |  |  |  |  |  |  |
| in the living room |  |  |  |  |  |  |
| he/she has gone out |  |  |  |  |  |  |

### Activity 2

Roy and Sylvia have a lot of things to do this weekend. Listen to them deciding which things they want to do. Put a tick in the correct column to show who does what.

|  | Roy | Sylvia | leave till later |
|---|---|---|---|
| clean the bathroom | ✓ |  |  |
| take out the rubbish |  |  |  |
| go shopping |  |  |  |
| clean the car |  |  |  |
| vacuum the carpet |  |  |  |
| clean the fridge |  |  |  |
| clean the windows |  |  |  |
| put away the groceries |  |  |  |
| iron the sheets |  |  |  |

## Activity 3

You are at home with your flatmate Virginia. Listen to what she says. What do you think she is going to ask you to do? Tick what you think she will ask.

1 ☑ Could you turn on the TV?
  ☐ Could you turn on the radio?

2 ☐ Could you get me something to drink?
  ☐ Could you get me something to eat?

3 ☐ Could you open the window?
  ☐ Could you close the window?

4 ☐ Could you turn on the lamp?
  ☐ Could you turn off the lamp?

5 ☐ Could you turn up the heating?
  ☐ Could you turn down the heating?

# Prices

There are three ways of saying prices and amounts of money in English. £8.50 can be said 'eight pounds and fifty pence', 'eight pounds fifty' and 'eight fifty'. In this unit you will hear all three ways. This will help you to learn and recognize them.

### Activity 1

Say these prices out loud.

| | | | | |
|---|---|---|---|---|
| £16.50 | £60.05 | £14.95 | £40.19 | £22.70 |
| £18.35 | £93.04 | £209.64 | £350.55 | £620.30 |
| £35,637 | £66,019 | £149,590 | £1,000,100 | |

Now listen to the tape and check that you said them correctly.

### Activity 2

Listen and tick the prices you hear.

1 ✓ £56.50
    £56.05

2 ☐ £11.07
    ☐ £11.17

3 ☐ £6.99
    ☐ £69.09

4 ☐ £167.07
    ☐ £1067.00

5 ☐ £119.45
    ☐ £109.45

6 ☐ £1980.00
    ☐ £198,000

7 ☐ £550.00
    ☐ £515.00

8 ☐ £1567.00
    ☐ £15,670.00

9 ☐ £175,900
    ☐ £125,900

10 ☐ £1,350,000
     ☐ £135,000

### Activity 3

Listen to the cashier add up these restaurant bills. Did he enter the correct prices? Put a tick or cross in each box.

**Gino's**   12 Leigh Hill Wootton   Tel: 34675

| | Price |
|---|---|
| starter | |
| main course | 11.15 |
| salad | 1.25 |
| drinks | 2.30 |
| dessert | 1.90 |
| Total | |

1 ☒

**Gino's**   12 Leigh Hill Wootton   Tel: 34675

| | Price |
|---|---|
| starter | 5.60 |
| main course | 20.70 |
| salad | |
| drinks | 6.15 |
| dessert | 14.05 |
| Total | |

2 ☐

**Gino's**   12 Leigh Hill Wootton   Tel: 34675

| | Price |
|---|---|
| starter | |
| main course | 5.75 |
| salad | 3.50 |
| drinks | 3.90 |
| dessert | 2.35 |
| Total | |

3 ☐

**Gino's**   12 Leigh Hill Wootton   Tel: 34675

| | Price |
|---|---|
| starter | |
| main course | 14.15 |
| salad | 3.00 |
| drinks | 7.80 |
| dessert | |
| Total | |

4 ☐

## Activity 4

Listen to a customs officer at Heathrow Airport asking David Carter how much he paid for the things he bought on holiday. Write the correct price next to each item and what its value is in pounds.

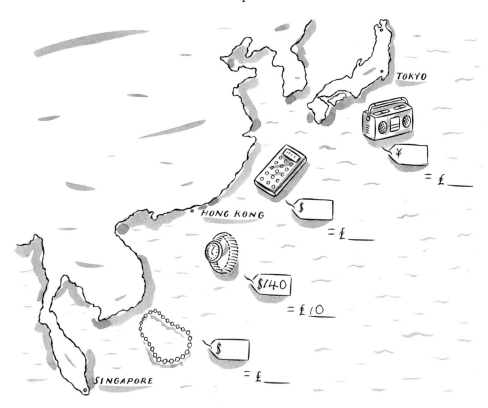

## Activity 5

Listen to people comparing the prices of things in three different cities. List the cities from the most expensive (1) to the least expensive (3).

| 1 | London | ..1... | 4 | Chicago | ...... |
|---|--------|--------|---|---------|--------|
| | Paris | ..2... | | San Francisco | ...... |
| | Madrid | ..3... | | Phoenix | ...... |
| 2 | New York | ...... | 5 | Mexico City | ...... |
| | London | ...... | | Los Angeles | ...... |
| | Tokyo | ...... | | Hong Kong | ...... |
| 3 | Singapore | ...... | 6 | Rio | ...... |
| | Tokyo | ...... | | Washington | ...... |
| | Honolulu | ...... | | Jakarta | ...... |

# Paying

## Activity 1

Listen to people paying for things in a department store. How do they pay for each item? Tick the correct box.

|  | Shopper 1 | Shopper 2 | Shopper 3 | Shopper 4 |
|---|---|---|---|---|
| Barclaycard |  |  |  |  |
| Access |  |  |  |  |
| American Express |  |  |  |  |
| personal cheque | ✓ |  |  |  |
| traveller's cheque |  |  |  |  |
| cash |  |  |  |  |

## Activity 2

Listen to people changing traveller's cheques at a bank. How much money do they want to change? How many of each kind of note do they want?

1 total = £  . . . . . .

  £5 notes  . . . . . .

  £10 notes  . . . . . .

  £20 notes  . . . . . .

  £50 notes  .✗.7..

2 total = £  . . . . . .

  £5 notes  . . . . . .

  £10 notes  . . . . . .

  £20 notes  . . . . . .

  £50 notes  . . . . . .

3 total = £  . . . . . .

  £5 notes  . . . . . .

  £10 notes  . . . . . .

  £20 notes  . . . . . .

  £50 notes  . . . . . .

4 total = £  . . . . . .

  £5 notes  . . . . . .

  £10 notes  . . . . . .

  £20 notes  . . . . . .

  £50 notes  . . . . . .

## Activity 3

Listen to people thinking about buying the things below. Will they buy the item, buy something else, or not buy anything? Tick what you think they will do.

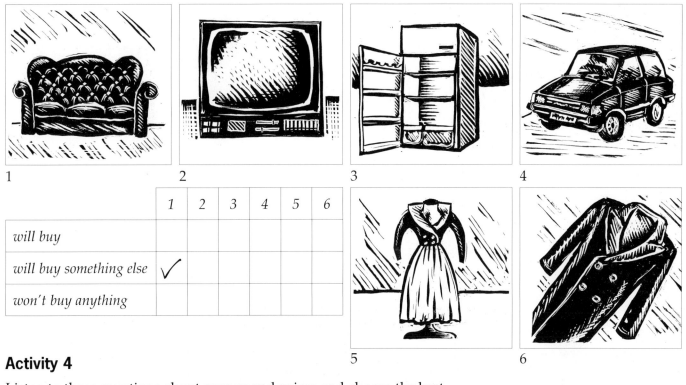

|  | 1 | 2 | 3 | 4 | 5 | 6 |
|---|---|---|---|---|---|---|
| *will buy* |  |  |  |  |  |  |
| *will buy something else* | ✓ |  |  |  |  |  |
| *won't buy anything* |  |  |  |  |  |  |

1

2

3

4

5

6

## Activity 4

Listen to these questions about money and prices and choose the best response.

1 ☑ It's only £45.
  ☐ Yes, I like it very much.

2 ☐ No, this is the cheapest.
  ☐ Yes, it is.

3 ☐ No, £1,550.
  ☐ No, I won't.

4 ☐ The green one.
  ☐ Not more than £50.

5 ☐ The ring's cheaper.
  ☐ The ring's very cheap.

6 ☐ £2.50 is enough.
  ☐ Yes, we should.

7 ☐ I'm sorry.
  ☐ Oh, did you?

8 ☐ Oh, I'm sorry. Let me check it again.
  ☐ That's OK.

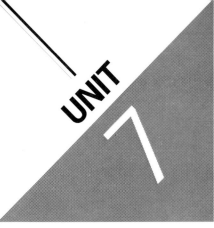

# Health

## Activity 1 *

Do you know these parts of the body? Match each word with the picture.

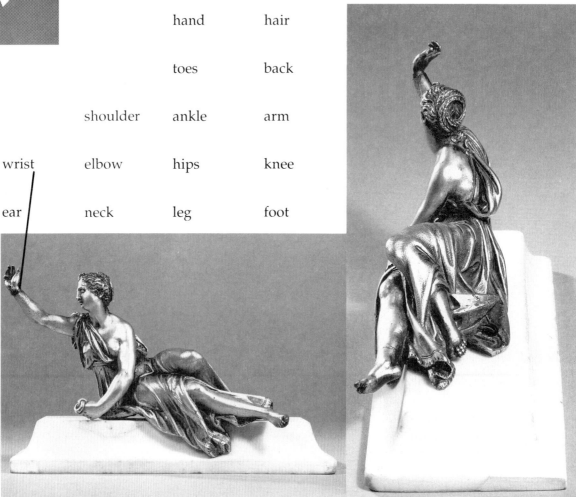

hand      hair

toes      back

shoulder      ankle      arm

wrist      elbow      hips      knee

ear      neck      leg      foot

fingers

eye

nose

lip

cheek

throat

chest

## Activity 2

You will hear sentences containing one of the words in each pair below.
Circle the word you hear.

| | | | |
|---|---|---|---|
| 1 toes | (nose) | 5 throat | foot |
| 2 neck | back | 6 wrist | chest |
| 3 hips | lips | 7 eyes | ears |
| 4 hair | ear | 8 leg | neck |

## Activity 3

You will hear people describing where they feel pain. Which part of the body are they describing? Number the parts described.

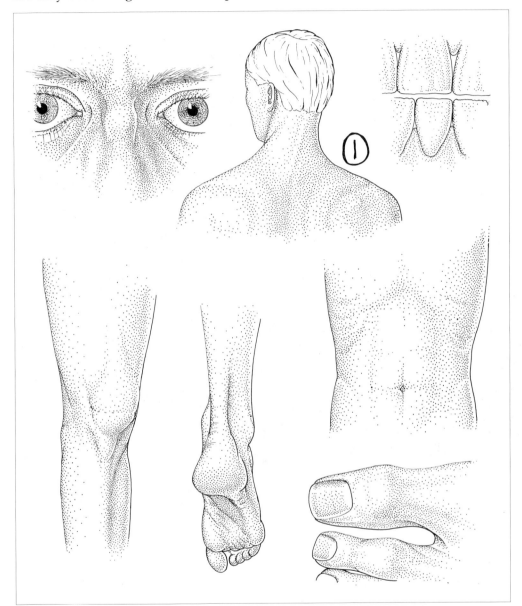

## Activity 4

Listen to these people describing how they feel. Number the sentences from 1-8 according to what is wrong with them.

. . . . . She's got toothache.                    . . . . . She's got a sore throat.

. . . . . She's got a headache.                   . . . . . He's got a sore foot.

. . . . . He's got earache.                       . . . . . She's got a stiff neck.

. . 1 . . He's got a cold.                        . . . . . He's got a sore finger.

## Activity 5

Listen to the doctor telling people what medicine to take. Write out what they have to take and how often each day. For example, if you hear, 'Take two and a half teaspoons every morning and evening', write 2½ tsp and × 2. If you hear, 'Take three of these tablets three times a day', write 3 tab and x 3.

*How much or how many?*        *How often each day?*

2½ tsp / 3 tab      X2 / X3

1 ......................................... .........................................

2 ......................................... .........................................

3 ......................................... .........................................

4 ......................................... .........................................

5 ......................................... .........................................

6 ......................................... .........................................

7 ......................................... .........................................

## Activity 6

How did these people hurt themselves? Listen and number the pictures 1 - 8.

a .....      b .....      c .....      d ..1..

e .....      f .....      g .....      h .....

## Activity 7

Listen to people talking about how they feel. Tick the best response.

1 ✓ Oh, that's good.
　☐ Oh, that's a pity.

2 ☐ Oh, that's great.
　☐ Oh, that's too bad.

3 ☐ Why did he do that?
　☐ How did he do that?

4 ☐ How do you feel?
　☐ Have you taken anything for it?

5 ☐ Why not?
　☐ What's the matter?

6 ☐ Oh, good.
　☐ What a pity!

7 ☐ What did you do?
　☐ Why don't you take something for it?

# Exercise

## Activity 1

How do these people keep fit? Listen and tick what they say.

1 ✓ swims regularly
　☐ goes climbing

2 ☐ runs
　☐ plays sports

3 ☐ exercises at work
　☐ walks

4 ☐ jogs
　☐ rides a bicycle

5 ☐ exercises regularly
　☐ plays sports

6 ☐ runs
　☐ rides a bicycle

7 ☐ plays sports
　☐ does daily exercise

# Describing objects

## Activity 1 *

Work on your own or in pairs. Read these advertisements for things people have lost. Match each description with a picture.

### Lost . . .

Lost near the Palace Theatre on the evening of 17.3.89 a digital ladies watch. Phone 236850. 5

Ladies handbag, black leather, no strap. In or around the central library. Please phone 389167. ☐

A pair of man's designer sunglasses with metal frames was dropped in the city park on Sunday afternoon (19.3. 89). If found, please phone Steve on 0622 55436. ☐

Small Japanese autofocus camera with case left on bus in Quarry Hill on Thursday afternoon (16.3. 89). Please write Box 25. ☐

Walkman with earphones and Tina Turner cassette inside lost near McDonalds on Saturday night. Phone 235460. ☐

Short-sleeved child's jumper dropped in the zoo. Phone 0432 26647. ☐

Lost: umbrella, black with curved handle. 234971. ☐

## Activity 2

Listen and circle the words you hear.

| | | | | | | |
|---|---|---|---|---|---|---|
| 1 | radio | (radios) | | 5 | watch | watches |
| 2 | shoe | shoes | | 6 | suitcase | suitcases |
| 3 | glass | glasses | | 7 | umbrella | umbrellas |
| 4 | brush | brushes | | 8 | bottle | bottles |

## Activity 3

You will hear people talking about seven of the things in the pictures below.
Number them from 1 - 7.

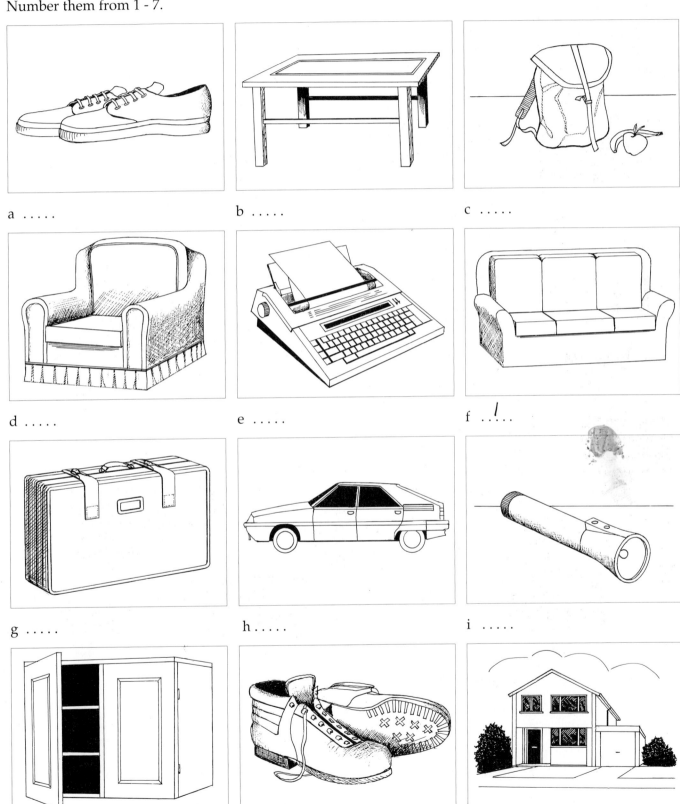

a . . . . .

b . . . . .

c . . . . .

d . . . . .

e . . . . .

f . . . . .

g . . . . .

h. . . . .

i . . . . .

j . . . . .

k . . . . .

l . . . . .

## Activity 4

You will hear people at a lost property office describing things they have lost. Circle a, b or c to identify the correct item for each person.

### Activity 5

Listen to people returning things to a department store. What is wrong with each item? Tick the best answer.

1 ....... too big ..✓.... too small

2 ....... sleeves too long ....... sleeves too short

3 ....... alarm doesn't work ....... doesn't keep correct time

4 ....... wrong key for lock ....... no key for lock

5 ....... earphones too small ....... earphones don't work

6 ....... doesn't open properly ....... doesn't close properly

7 ....... light isn't working ....... no battery

# Describing people

### Activity 1

You will hear people describing someone they are looking for at a party.
Listen and number the people correctly from 1 - 7.

## Activity 2

You will hear people talking about their families. Listen and write the correct name under each member of the families.

1 Tracy
Jenny
Paul
Kevin

2 Karen
Ellen
me
Dad
David

3 Fred
Susan
Dick
Margaret

## Activity 3

You will hear sentences about different people. If the sentence sounds like this:

*She's wearing a green blouse.*

the speaker is making a statement. If the sentence sounds like this:

*She's wearing a green blouse?*

the speaker is asking a question. Listen and tick under statement or question.

|   | statement | question |   | statement | question |
|---|-----------|----------|---|-----------|----------|
| 1 | ✓ | ........ | 5 | ........ | ........ |
| 2 | ........ | ........ | 6 | ........ | ........ |
| 3 | ........ | ........ | 7 | ........ | ........ |
| 4 | ........ | ........ | 8 | ........ | ........ |

# Shops and shopping

## Activity 1

Look at this shopping list. Write each item on the list next to the shop where you buy it.

| Shopping list | |
|---|---|
| dog food | |
| frying pan | |
| weekend groceries | |
| stamps | |
| paint | |
| tennis shoes | |
| bread and cakes | |
| soft drinks | |
| coffee table | |
| photography magazine | |
| ladder | |
| wine | |
| newspaper | |
| garden tools | |
| paperback | |

bookshop . . . . . . . . . . . . . . . . . . . . . . . . . . .

supermarket . . . . . . . . . . . . . . . . . . . . . . . . . . . . . .

florist . . . . . . . . . . . . . . . . . . . . . . . . . . . . . . . . .

hardware store . . . . . . . . . . . . . . . . . . . . . . . . . . . . .

pet shop . . . *dog food* . . . . . . . . . . . . . . . . . . . . . . .

furniture shop . . . . . . . . . . . . . . . . . . . . . . . . . . . . .

off-licence . . . . . . . . . . . . . . . . . . . . . . . . . . . . . .

post office . . . . . . . . . . . . . . . . . . . . . . . . . . . . . . .

bakery . . . . . . . . . . . . . . . . . . . . . . . . . . . . . . . . .

sports shop . . . . . . . . . . . . . . . . . . . . . . . . . . . . . .

newsagent . . . . . . . . . . . . . . . . . . . . . . . . . . . . . . .

Now underline the stressed syllable in all the items with more than one syllable. Then listen to the tape and check that you have marked them correctly.

## Activity 2

Shirley and Roger are talking about the things they have got to do when they are out. Tick the places they will go to on the list below.

| | |
|---|---|
| ☐ off-licence | ☐ furniture shop |
| ☐ hardware store | ☐ bakery |
| ✓ post office | ☐ pet shop |
| ☐ florist | |

## Activity 3

Roger is going to the supermarket. He's checking the things below in the kitchen. Listen and decide whether there's a lot, a little, or none at all. Tick the correct box.

| | bread | butter | milk | eggs | sugar | vegetables | cooking oil | ketchup |
|---|---|---|---|---|---|---|---|---|
| a lot | | | | | | | | |
| a little/a few | ✓ | | | | | | | |
| none at all | | | | | | | | |

## Activity 4

Shirley and Roger are deciding where to buy some of the things they need. They will go to one of the places below. Listen and tick the name of the shop they are going to.

1 ☑ Ace Supermarket
☐ Star Supermarket

2 ☐ King's Bakery
☐ West's Bakery

3 ☐ Betty's Flower Shop
☐ Regal Florist

4 ☐ Crest Hardware
☐ Ted's Hardware

5 ☐ Hill's Bookshop
☐ University Bookshop

6 ☐ Liberty Department Store
☐ Ellis's Department Store

7 ☐ Mullins Greengrocers
☐ Hollins Greengrocers

Now listen again. Why did they decide to go to the shops they chose? Tick the reasons below.

1 ☐ good prices
☑ easy to park

2 ☐ cheaper
☐ bread is fresher

3 ☐ friendly staff
☐ better prices

4 ☐ the shop has a sale on
☐ more choice

5 ☐ cheaper prices
☐ better books

6 ☐ a nicer shop
☐ the other shop is not open

7 ☐ better prices
☐ better vegetables

## Activity 5

Some of the items below are for sale in a newspaper. Listen to people phoning to ask questions about them. Number the eight things talked about from 1 - 8. Then listen again. How old is each thing? Tick the correct box.

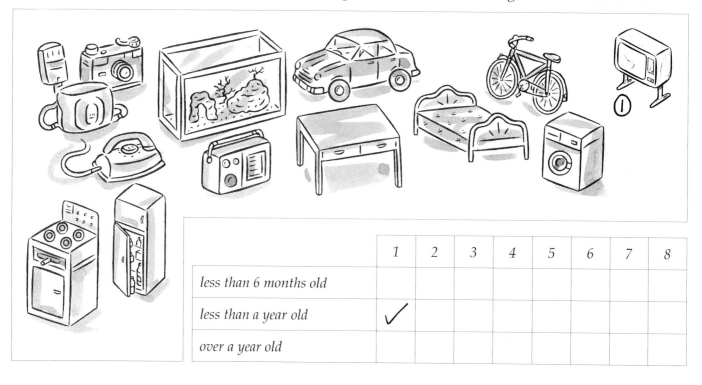

|  | 1 | 2 | 3 | 4 | 5 | 6 | 7 | 8 |
|---|---|---|---|---|---|---|---|---|
| *less than 6 months old* |  |  |  |  |  |  |  |  |
| *less than a year old* | ✓ |  |  |  |  |  |  |  |
| *over a year old* |  |  |  |  |  |  |  |  |

## Activity 6

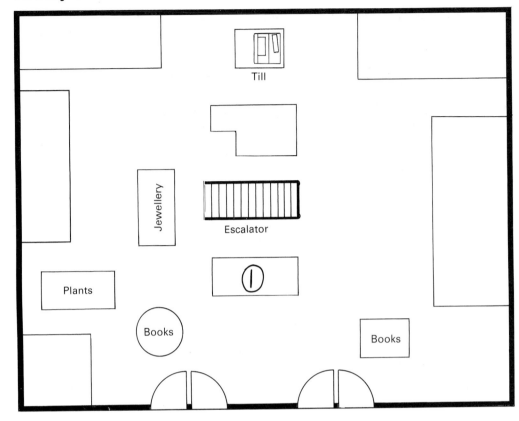

Listen to people asking where places are in a department store. Mark each of these places.

1 toy section
2 magazine section
3 sports department
4 menswear
5 women's clothes
6 kitchenware
7 cosmetics

## Activity 7

You will hear people buying presents. Listen and decide what you think they will buy. Tick the correct item.

1 ☐ a record
  ☐ a bracelet
  ✓ some perfume

2 ☐ some socks
  ☐ a sweater
  ☐ a scarf

3 ☐ the red blouse
  ☐ the yellow blouse
  ☐ the green blouse

4 ☐ the toy lorry
  ☐ the toy tank
  ☐ the toy car

5 ☐ the dish
  ☐ the plate
  ☐ the vase

6 ☐ the bracelet
  ☐ the necklace
  ☐ the ear-rings

7 ☐ the soap
  ☐ the aftershave
  ☐ the cologne

# Going on holiday

## Activity 1 *

What do you like doing when you are on holiday and visiting a city for the first time? List the activities below from most important (1) to least important (9). Then compare with your partner.

...... going to museums ...... visiting the nightclubs

...... going to art galleries ...... going to the theatre

...... going shopping ...... going to discos

...... trying the local food ...... taking photographs

...... sightseeing

## Activity 2

Listen to these people on holiday planning what they are going to do. Number what you hear from 1 - 5.

...... go shopping

...... visit a museum or art gallery

...1... go sightseeing

...... go to a restaurant

...... go to a nightclub

## Activity 3

Listen to people talking about their holidays. What places did they visit?
Tick the places they visited in each list below.

1
☑ Thailand
☑ Hong Kong
☐ China
☑ Japan
☐ Korea

2
☐ Greece
☐ Holland
☐ Italy
☐ Spain
☐ France

3
☐ Chicago
☐ Los Angeles
☐ Boston
☐ Washington
☐ New York
☐ San Francisco

4
☐ Brussels
☐ Rome
☐ Vienna
☐ Naples
☐ Paris
☐ Munich

## Activity 4

Listen to people talking about different cities. What can you do in each
place? Tick the lists below.

1
☐ go shopping
☑ go for a walk
☐ drive around
☑ try the local food
☐ visit a museum or art gallery

2
☐ go swimming
☐ take a boat trip
☐ go skiing
☐ go round the island by bus
☐ try the local food

3
☐ visit the old castle
☐ go shopping
☐ visit the hotels
☐ go to the nightclubs
☐ go swimming

4
☐ visit the museums
☐ go to the theatre
☐ go to a nightclub
☐ try Chinese food
☐ try the local food

**Activity 5**

Listen to people getting ready for their holidays. Tick the things they are going to take with them.

1    large suitcase      2    large suitcase
   ✓ small suitcase          small suitcase
     presents             presents
     camera              camera
     personal stereo       personal stereo
     books               books
     swimsuit            swimsuit
     umbrella            umbrella
     coat                coat
     medicine            medicine

**Activity 6**

Listen to people talking about their holidays. Did they enjoy themselves? Tick the best answer.

|  | 1 | 2 | 3 | 4 | 5 | 6 | 7 |
|---|---|---|---|---|---|---|---|
| *liked everything* | ✓ | | | | | | |
| *liked some things* | | | | | | | |
| *didn't like anything* | | | | | | | |

**Activity 7**

Listen to questions about travel and choose the best answer.

1    Yes, I did.       5    Last week.
   ✓ Very much, thanks.      Not yet.

2    For about six weeks.    6    Not yet.
     Yes, I will.            No, I didn't.

3    Not really.         7    Yes, I was.
     Until June.           About a month.

4    Yes, I did.        8    It was great.
     To Madrid.           Yes, I did.

# Transport

## Activity 1 *

Work in pairs. Can you name these different kinds of transport?

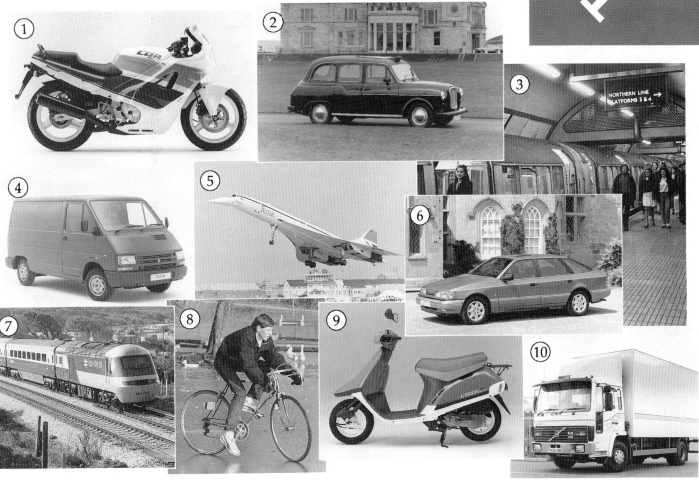

## Activity 2

You will hear sentences containing one of the phrases below. Tick the phrase you hear.

1 ☐ a new moped
  ☑ a <u>blue</u> moped

2 ☐ an old sports car
  ☐ a gold sports car

3 ☐ a light blue van
  ☐ a bright blue van

4 ☐ a green bus
  ☐ a grey bus

5 ☐ the green train
  ☐ the green plane

6 ☐ the last train
  ☐ the fast train

7 ☐ a dark brown Mini
  ☐ a dark green Mini

8 ☐ a dark blue Toyota
  ☐ a light blue Toyota

Now underline the stressed word in each answer. Then listen again to check that you marked them correctly.

## Activity 3

You will hear people describing their transport. Tick the correct box, a or b.

1a ☐ b ☑     2a ☐ b ☐

 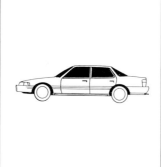  

3a ☐ b ☐     4a ☐ b ☐

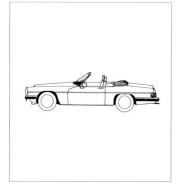   

5a ☐ b ☐     6a ☐ b ☐

## Activity 4

You will hear people asking about buses from the bus station to the place below. What number bus or buses can they take and how often do the buses go? If a bus goes every 20 minutes, write 20 mins under 'frequency'.

| Destination | bus/es | frequency |
| --- | --- | --- |
| zoo | 17 or 24 | 20 mins. |
| airport | | |
| museum | | |
| university | | |
| hospital | | |
| library | | |

## Activity 5

You will hear people talking to a taxi driver. Where does each passenger want to go? Number the places 1 - 6.

. . . . . . library         . . . . . . museum         . . . . . . university

. . . . . . zoo         . . . . . . department store         . . .1. . airport

. . . . . . hospital         . . . . . . restaurant         . . . . . . theatre

# Street directions

## Activity 1

You will hear visitors in a city asking where places are. Listen and circle the place which is closer to the speakers.

1   (Bank of Scotland)   4   Royal Hotel
    Clydesdale Bank          Rose Hotel

2   Star Supermarket     5   Natural History Museum
    Everfresh Supermarket    Museum of Modern Art

3   Palace Restaurant    6   Mediterranean Travel
    Hong Kong Restaurant     National Travel

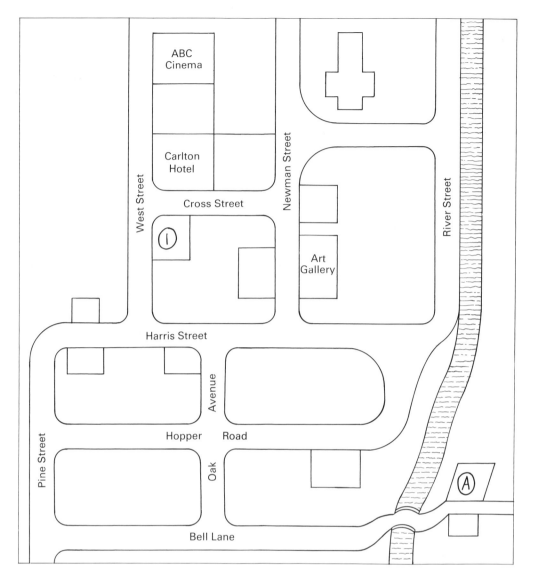

## Activity 2

You will hear people asking where the places below are. Number the correct places on the map.

1 chemist
2 post office
3 bookshop
4 supermarket
5 petrol station
6 bus stop

## Activity 3

Listen to people being given directions to the places below. Mark the directions on the map and write in the correct letter for the places they are looking for.

A Star Hotel
B bank
C hairdresser
D supermarket
E travel agent
F dry cleaner

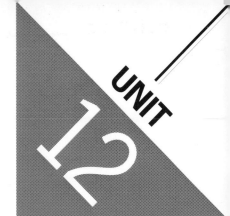

# Jobs

## Activity 1

Look at these occupations. Choose the five that you would find most interesting. List them from 1 - 5. Then compare your list with your partner's.

| | | |
|---|---|---|
| accountant | doctor | nurse |
| architect | engineer | pilot |
| bank clerk | estate agent | police officer |
| car mechanic | hairdresser | receptionist |
| cashier | journalist | sales assistant |
| computer programmer | librarian | secretary |
| dentist | lorry driver | social worker |
| designer | model | university lecturer |

Do you know how to pronounce these occupations correctly? Listen to the tape and then underline the stressed syllables.

## Activity 2

You will hear people describing some of the things they do at work. Listen and tick the activities they describe.

1 ✓ interview people
      describe people

2    collect guests
      take guests on tours

3    fill in forms
      type letters

4    sell houses
      buy houses

5    collect post
      deliver post

6    sell TV sets
      repair TV sets

7    check machines
      mend machines

8    take telephone calls
      make telephone calls

## Activity 3

You will hear people talking about their occupations. Listen and number six of the occupations below from 1 - 6.

| | | | |
|---|---|---|---|
| . . . . . . | typist | . . . . . . | mechanic |
| . . . . . . | hairdresser | . . . . . . | nurse |
| . . . . . . | actor | . . . . . . | pilot |
| . . . . . . | engineer | . . . . . . | university lecturer |
| . . . . . . | hotel receptionist | . . . . . . | computer programmer |

## Activity 4

You will hear people talking about the jobs they used to have and the jobs they have now. Listen and tick their present job.

1 ☑ nurse
   ☐ social worker

2 ☐ shop assistant
   ☐ librarian

3 ☐ driver
   ☐ tour guide

4 ☐ receptionist
   ☐ nurse

5 ☐ bank clerk
   ☐ computer programmer

6 ☐ mechanic
   ☐ lorry driver

7 ☐ office manager
   ☐ university lecturer

## Activity 5

You will hear Ms Patel telling her secretary what she wants her to do today. Listen and number five of the activities below from 1 - 5 in the order she talks about them.

| | | | |
|---|---|---|---|
| . . . . . . | post a package | . .1. . . | arrange a meeting |
| . . . . . . | type a report | . . . . . . | check the sales figures |
| . . . . . . | collect some tickets | . . . . . . | make travel arrangements |
| . . . . . . | copy a letter | . . . . . . | cancel an appointment |

## Activity 6

Jane is starting a new job in an office. Helen is showing her where things are in the stationery cupboard. Listen and number the correct place in the picture.

1 letter paper
2 envelopes
3 pens
4 notebooks
5 elastic bands
6 sellotape

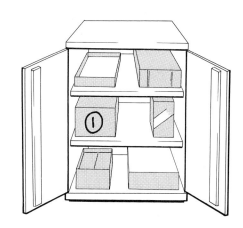

## Activity 7

Listen to people asking where places are in an office block. Each person is at X. Number the correct places.

1 coffee bar
2 accounts department
3 manager's office
4 toilet
5 Mr Smith's office
6 stationery store
7 Ms Randall's office
8 photocopier
9 post room

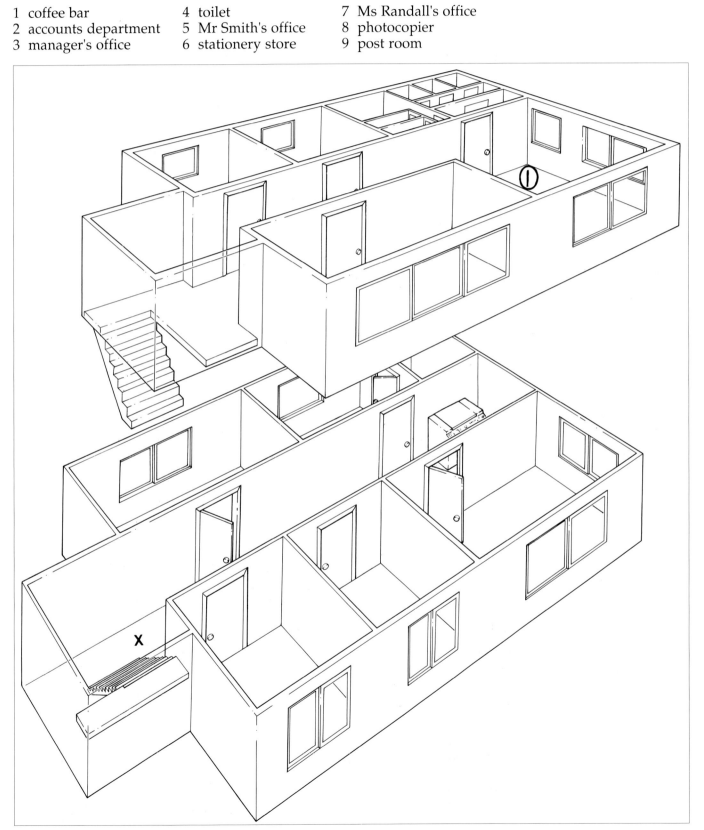

# Leaving messages

### Activity 1

Listen to people ringing an office to ask to speak to someone. The person is not in. Tick what the callers do.

|  | 1 | 2 | 3 | 4 | 5 | 6 |
|---|---|---|---|---|---|---|
| leave a message |  |  |  |  |  |  |
| make an appointment |  |  |  |  |  |  |
| call back later |  |  |  |  |  |  |
| wait | ✓ |  |  |  |  |  |
| ask to speak to someone else |  |  |  |  |  |  |

# Job interviews

### Activity 1

Listen to four people being interviewed for jobs. Tick the correct information below.

|  |  | 1 | 2 | 3 | 4 |
|---|---|---|---|---|---|
| education | secondary school | ✓ |  |  |  |
|  | college/university |  |  |  |  |
| the job | office job |  |  |  |  |
|  | factory job |  |  |  |  |
|  | shop assistant |  |  |  |  |
|  | hospital job |  |  |  |  |
|  | hotel job |  |  |  |  |
| previous experience | a lot |  |  |  |  |
|  | some |  |  |  |  |
|  | none |  |  |  |  |

## Activity 2

You will hear questions from a job interview. Listen and choose the best answer to each question.

1 ☑ I was a student.
   ☐ Three months ago.

2 ☐ Not quite.
   ☐ Yes, I have.

3 ☐ Quite well.
   ☐ Two.

4 ☐ Not very well.
   ☐ Yes, I can.

5 ☐ In Edinburgh.
   ☐ From 1982 to 1986.

6 ☐ In London.
   ☐ Three.

7 ☐ Two years.
   ☐ In 1986.

8 ☐ £150 a week.
   ☐ Yes, it was.

## UNIT 13

# Leisure activities

### Activity 1*

How much time do you usually spend on these activities each weekend? Are there other ways you spend your weekend? Tick the responses below. Then compare your responses with your partner's.

|  | a little | some | a lot |
|---|---|---|---|
| reading the newspaper |  |  |  |
| reading books or magazines |  |  |  |
| watching TV |  |  |  |
| listening to the radio |  |  |  |
| cleaning the house |  |  |  |
| cooking |  |  |  |
| studying |  |  |  |
| writing letters |  |  |  |
| talking on the telephone |  |  |  |
| other activities |  |  |  |

### Activity 2

You will hear short telephone conversations. What was each person doing when the phone rang? Number six of the pictures below from 1 - 6.

a . . . . .

b . . . . .

c . . . . .

d . . . . .

e . . . . .

f . . . . .

g . .l. . .

h . . . . .

## Activity 3

You will hear people talking about the things they like and don't like doing in their spare time. Listen and tick how much they like each activity.

|  | likes it a lot | likes it a little | doesn't like it at all |
|---|---|---|---|
| 1 playing cards |  | ✓ |  |
| 2 playing sports |  |  |  |
| 3 going to parties |  |  |  |
| 4 eating out |  |  |  |
| 5 dancing |  |  |  |
| 6 watching TV |  |  |  |
| 7 listening to music |  |  |  |
| 8 cooking |  |  |  |

### Activity 4

Listen to people getting ready to do something. Tick what you think they are going to do.

1 ☑ go swimming       5 ☐ watch TV
   ☐ go for a drive          ☐ listen to the radio

2 ☐ go to the cinema      6 ☐ go to a party
   ☐ go to a restaurant      ☐ have friends round for dinner

3 ☐ go to a concert       7 ☐ go to a barbecue
   ☐ go dancing            ☐ go to a restaurant

4 ☐ play tennis
   ☐ play basketball

### Activity 5

You will hear people talking about things they have done. Listen and tick how much they enjoyed them.

|   | liked everything | liked some things | didn't like anything |
|---|---|---|---|
| 1 |  | ✓ |  |
| 2 |  |  |  |
| 3 |  |  |  |
| 4 |  |  |  |
| 5 |  |  |  |
| 6 |  |  |  |
| 7 |  |  |  |

# Invitations and arrangements

### Activity 1

You will hear people inviting a friend to go somewhere with them. Listen and tick whether they said 'yes' or 'no'.

|   | said yes | said no |   |   | said yes | said no |
|---|---|---|---|---|---|---|
| 1 | ...... | ✓ |  | 5 | ...... | ...... |
| 2 | ...... | ...... |  | 6 | ...... | ...... |
| 3 | ...... | ...... |  | 7 | ...... | ...... |
| 4 | ...... | ...... |  |  |  |  |

## Activity 2

Listen to people arranging to do something. What are they going to do? Write down the day they will meet and the time.

Monday = Mon       Friday = Fri
Tuesday = Tue       Saturday = Sat
Wednesday = Wed     Sunday = Sun
Thursday = Thu

|  | 1 | | 2 | | 3 | | 4 | |
|---|---|---|---|---|---|---|---|---|
|  | day | time | day | time | day | time | day | time |
| film |  |  |  |  |  |  |  |  |
| restaurant |  |  |  |  |  |  |  |  |
| party |  |  |  |  |  |  |  |  |
| disco | Sat | 9p.m. |  |  |  |  |  |  |
| picnic |  |  |  |  |  |  |  |  |

## Activity 3

Choose the best response to the questions you hear.

1 ☑ Not really.
  ☐ No, thanks.

2 ☐ Yes, I have.
  ☐ It's OK.

3 ☐ Yes, I did.
  ☐ It was interesting.

4 ☐ Quite a bit.
  ☐ Yes, I can.

5 ☐ Sorry, I'm not free.
  ☐ Yes, I am.

6 ☐ Yes, I can.
  ☐ Not really.

7 ☐ Fine, thanks.
  ☐ Yes, it was.

8 ☐ No, thanks.
  ☐ Yes, it was great.

## UNIT 14

# Instructions

### Activity 1*

How do you use a coin-operated washing machine? Work in pairs and describe how to use a machine like the one shown below. Use phrases like these:

First you . . .
Then you . . .
Next you . . .

You may want to use these verbs.

put in   add   turn on   take out

### Activity 2

Listen to people describing how to use different pieces of equipment. Number the things they talk about in the correct order, from 1 - 4.

a . . . . .

b . 1 . . .

c . . . . .

d . . . . .

### Activity 3

You will hear a recipe for chicken cooked with aubergine, garlic, sauce, and herbs. Listen to the instructions and number eight of the sentences from 1 - 8.

Add the water.

1 | Cut up the garlic.

Cook it for ten minutes.

Add the sauce and herbs.

Fry the chicken and aubergine.

Fry the garlic.

Cut up the chicken.

Cut up the aubergine.

## Activity 4

You will hear a sales assistant telling a customer how to look after some of the things below. Number six of them from 1 - 6 in the order in which you hear them.

a . . . . .          b . . . . .          c . .1. . .          d . . . . .

e . . . . .          f . . . . .          g . . . . .

h . . . . .          i . . . . .          j . . . . .          k . . . . .

## Activity 5

Listen to a sales assistant telling someone how to clean and look after different things. Tick the advice the sales assistant gives.

1 ☑ handwash only
  ☐ machine wash only

2 ☐ handwash only
  ☐ machine wash only

3 ☐ wash in warm water
  ☐ wash in hot water

4 ☐ dry clean only
  ☐ do not dry clean

5 ☐ iron
  ☐ do not iron

6 ☐ clean with oil
  ☐ clean with soap and water

7 ☐ wash in washing machine
  ☐ wash by hand

8 ☐ wash in dishwasher
  ☐ wash by hand

## Activity 6

Listen to these customers saying what they need done. Tick what they want.

1 ☐ cut very short
  ☑ not cut much

2 ☐ cut only
  ☐ cut and shampoo

3 ☐ washed and mended
  ☐ washed only

4 ☐ full tank of petrol
  ☐ £5 of petrol

5 ☐ repaired and painted
  ☐ repaired

6 ☐ polished and checked
  ☐ checked only

7 ☐ repaired
  ☐ repaired and painted

8 ☐ cleaned
  ☐ cleaned and new strap put on

9 ☐ heeled and soled
  ☐ heeled only

## Activity 7

Mrs Potter is asking her children to do things. She wants them to do some things now and some things later. Tick what she wants them to do first.

1 ☑ iron the clothes
  ☐ make the beds

2 ☐ wash the dishes
  ☐ tidy the living room

3 ☐ water the plants
  ☐ clean the cooker

4 ☐ cut up the meat
  ☐ cut up the vegetables

5 ☐ do the dishes
  ☐ clean the windows

6 ☐ vacuum the floor
  ☐ polish the table

7 ☐ tidy the bedrooms
  ☐ clean the bathroom

## Activity 8

Your flatmate Elaine likes moving things around in your flat. Listen to her deciding what to change. Draw a line from each item to its new position. She makes six changes.

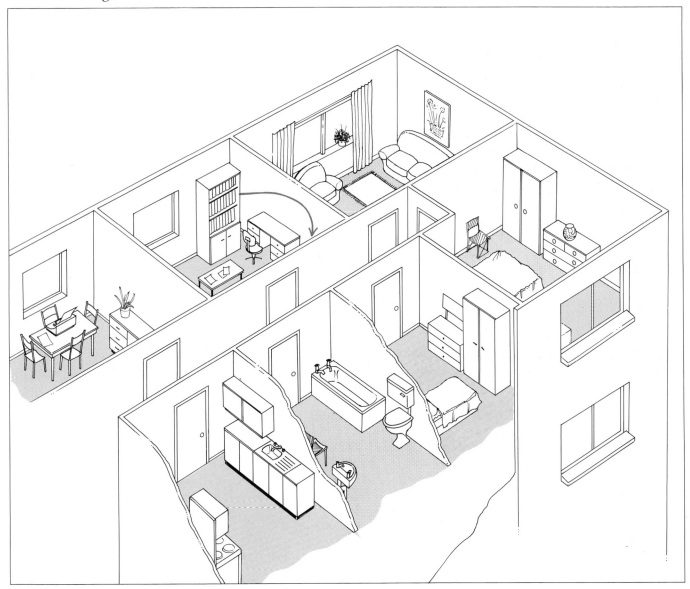

# Airports

## Activity 1 *

At an airport where do we go to do the following? Complete the table.

| | |
|---|---|
| **Information desk** | ↑ |
| **Duty-free shop** | ↓ |
| **Restaurant** | ↑ |
| **Check-in** | → |
| **Departure lounge** | ↑ |
| **Arrivals** | → |
| **Customs** | ↑ |
| **Bank** | → |
| **Post office** | → |
| **Snack bar** | ↑ |

declare taxable goods .......... *Customs* ..................................

meet a friend who has just arrived ....................................

wait to board the plane ..............................................

buy tax-free goods ..................................................

get the seat number for a flight ......................................

have a meal .........................................................

have a sandwich .....................................................

find out about sightseeing ...........................................

change some money ..................................................

send a postcard ......................................................

## Activity 2

You will hear sentences containing some of the places below. Number the places you hear from 1 - 7.

..... departure gate ..... departure lounge ..... telephone booth

..... post office ..1... immigration ..... information desk

..... restaurant ..... post box

Now underline the stressed syllables. Listen again to check you marked them correctly.

## Activity 3

Listen to airport announcements for the people below. Match each name with the correct announcement.

1 Fiona Johnson  4 Linda Kennedy
2 Yau Chit Man  5 Henri Bourassa
3 Hisashi Uematsu  6 Jean Halpern

... report to information desk  ... go to Singapore Airlines desk

... a telephone call for you  ... go to Japan Airlines ticket counter

... message at Air France desk  ... go to immigrations and customs

... go to the meeting point  ... go to Cathay Pacific check-in counter

## Activity 4

Listen to these airport announcements and complete the missing information about each flight.

|   | flight | departure time | gate |
|---|--------|----------------|------|
| 1 | BA445 | 20.35 | 16 |
| 2 | BA116 | | |
| 3 | | 15.25 | |
| 4 | | | 12 |
| 5 | JAL176 | | |
| 6 | | | 3 |
| 7 | | 11.15 | |

## Activity 5

The people below have just arrived at the airport. They want different kinds of hotel accommodation. They each dial a hotel and receive a recorded message. Listen to the message and tick what you think each caller will do next.

1 ☐ make a reservation
  ✓ try a different hotel

2 ☐ make a reservation
  ☐ try a different hotel

3 ☐ make a reservation
  ☐ try a different hotel

4 ☐ make a reservation
  ☐ try a different hotel

5 ☐ make a reservation
  ☐ try a different hotel

6 ☐ make a reservation
  ☐ try a different hotel

## Activity 6

You will hear people who have just arrived at an airport phoning friends. Their friends are out. They leave a message on their friend's answering machine. Tick the messages they leave.

1 ☐ will call again today
  ☐ wants a place to stay
  ✓ called to say 'Hello.'

2 ☐ wants a place to stay
  ☐ staying at a hotel
  ☐ staying with friends

3 ☐ call me at my hotel
  ☐ visit me at my hotel
  ☐ will call you later at the hotel

4 ☐ in town for a day
  ☐ in town for three or four days
  ☐ in town for a week

5 ☐ will meet you tonight
  ☐ will meet you tomorrow night
  ☐ wants to meet you at the weekend

6 ☐ will have dinner with you at your home
  ☐ invites you to the hotel for dinner
  ☐ invites you out to dinner

# Immigration

## Activity 1

You will hear questions asked by a customs or immigration officer at the airport. Tick the best answer to each question.

1 ☐ No, I haven't.
 ✓ For a month.

2 ☐ To see friends.
 ☐ I'm a technician.

3 ☐ $18,000 a year.
 ☐ $1,500.

4 ☐ With friends.
 ☐ For a month.

5 ☐ At 2.30.
 ☐ SQ 250.

6 ☐ No, I'm alone.
 ☐ Yes, we were.

7 ☐ No, thanks.
 ☐ Here it is.

8 ☐ No, it isn't.
 ☐ The brown one.

# UNIT 1

## Numbers

### Activity 1 (2' 05")

| | |
|---|---|
| five | nine hundred and twenty-five |
| seventeen | one thousand and three |
| twenty-seven | one thousand and twelve |
| eighty-nine | one thousand one hundred and twenty |
| seven | one thousand three hundred and seventy-six |
| thirty | one thousand five hundred and thirty-nine |
| thirty-nine | one thousand six hundred and thirty |
| fifty-one | one thousand seven hundred and eighty |
| eighty | one thousand eight hundred and ninety-nine |
| one hundred and twenty | one thousand nine hundred and five |
| three hundred and forty-nine | |
| four hundred and nine | |
| four hundred and eleven | |
| five hundred and seventy-nine | |
| six hundred and fourteen | |
| seven hundred and thirty-two | |

### Activity 2 (45")

You will hear seven numbers. Circle the numbers you hear.

1 twenty-two
2 one hundred and ninety
3 thirteen
4 one thousand and ten
5 seventy
6 one hundred and fifty-one
7 one thousand five hundred and fifty nine

### Activity 3 (1' 52")

Listen to the prizes in a lottery. What were the winning numbers? Circle the correct number for each prize.

And here are the prizes in the lottery. Has everybody got their tickets? Good. Well, the seventh prize is ticket number one hundred and fifteen. A hundred and fifteen. The sixth prize is . . . number one thousand seven hundred and seventy. One thousand seven hundred and seventy. The fifth prize goes to ticket number nineteen, nineteen. Now, let's see who'll win the fourth prize.

Mmmm . . . it looks like, yes, number three hundred and nine. Three hundred and nine is the lucky number. Now, we have three more prizes. OK. The third prize goes to ticket number fifty-nine. Fifty-nine. Right, and second prize goes to ticket number one thousand nine hundred and ninety. Who has ticket number one thousand nine hundred and ninety in second place? Finally, the first prize. The lucky first prize winner is ticket number forty. Number forty wins the first prize!

## Telephone Numbers

### Activity 1 (1' 10")

oh eight three oh, nine four one, double five seven
oh one, three oh eight, double three seven eight
oh two seven four, three double eight two six
oh five one, four three, three seven eight
oh six one, three five two, two eight double nine
eight six, four five one, two eight three
oh two one, six one six, seven four two five
oh four six two, six two three, seven two eight

### Activity 2 (1' 29")

You will hear nine telephone numbers. Tick the numbers you hear.

| 1 | 313597 | 4 | 0519 23092 | 7 | 068 91 789 |
|---|---|---|---|---|---|
| 2 | 743678 | 5 | 0457 64332 | 8 | 339279 |
| 3 | 01 808 7688 | 6 | 041 904 5308 | 9 | 0425 5781 |

### Activity 4 (2' 18")

Listen to people asking Directory Enquiries for telephone numbers for the places below. Write down the correct numbers.

1
A Directory enquiries, which town please?
B Oxford.
A What name?
B I'd like the number of the John Radcliffe hospital, please.
A John Radcliffe hospital.
(pause)
The number's Oxford 64711
B Thank you.

2
A Directory enquiries, which town please?
B Birmingham.
A What name?
B The Odeon Cinema, please.
A Odeon Cinema.
(pause)
Yes, The number's 021 930 2738
B Thanks, bye.

3
A Directory enquiries, which town please?
B Manchester, please.
A What name?

B  Could I have the number for the Shangri-La resaurant?
A  Shangri-La, yes . . . the number is 061 439 4576

4
A  Directory enquiries, which town please?
B  London.
A  What name?
B  London University, please.
A  University of London.
   (pause)
   The number's 01 388 0542
B  Thank you.

5
A  Directory enquiries, which town please?
B  Bristol, please.
A  What name?
B  I'd like the number for County Hall.
A  County Hall.
   (pause)
   Bristol 88070

6
A  Directory enquiries, which town please?
B  Edinburgh
A  What name?
B  British Airways office.
A  British Airways, yes, the number's 031 897 4567.
B  Thank you. Bye.

## Activity 5 (1' 22")

Listen to people telephoning the places below. Did they dial the right number or not? Tick the correct box, right or wrong.

1  Let me see. The number for the restaurant is 0439 7889.
2  Now, the number for the Central Library is 35946.
3  The number for the Inland Revenue is 40811.
4  I'll call the bookshop. The number is 01 636 1577.
5  British Caledonian. That's 0759 41112.
6  The number for Kim's Food Store is 021 876 3804.

# Addresses

## Activity 1 (1' 16")

Listen to people asking for the addresses of these places. Tick the correct address.

1  A  What's the address of American Express?
   B  It's 89 Mount Street.
2  A  Could I have the address of Asia Pacific Travel, please?
   B  The address is 103 Waterloo Road.
3  A  Do you have the address of Black and Decker?
   B  Yes, their address is 623 Holloway Road.
4  A  I wonder if you could give me the address of Gulf House?
   B  Yes, the address is 2 Portman Street, W1.
5  A  What's the address of Pan American, please?
   B  It's 193 Piccadilly.

6  A  Where's the Eastman Dental Hospital?
   B  It's at 256 Grays Inn Road.

## Activity 2 (1')

Listen to people giving their addresses. Complete the missing information.

1  A  What's your address?
   B  Three hundred and thirteen Cumberland Avenue.
2  A  Whereabouts on University Drive do you live?
   B  At six hundred and fifteen, flat nineteen.
3  A  Could I have your address, please?
   B  Yes, I live at 59 Wellington Street.
4  A  Could you give me your address?
   B  Yes, it's Grant Street. A hundred and nine Grant Street.
5  A  You live on Judd Street, don't you?
   B  Yes, I'm at two hundred and six Judd Street, flat fifteen.

# UNIT 2

# Names

## Activity 1 (1' 08")

| George | Jones | Richards | Simpson | Thomson |
|--------|-------|----------|---------|---------|
| Gordon | Johnson | Richmond | Samson | Thomas |
| Gray | Harris | Short | Schmidt | Winters |
| Graham | Harrison | Shaw | Smith | Wilson |

## Activity 2 (56")

Some of the people from Activity 1 will give their names. Number the names you hear from 1 - 8.

1  My name's Short. Bill Short.
2  I'm Fiona Thomas.
3  Tina Johnson.
4  My name's Gray.
5  I'm Kim Richmond.
6  My name's Gloria Simpson.
7  Heather Jones is my name.
8  I'm David Smith.

## Activity 5 (3' 30")

Listen to people opening bank accounts. Write down their names.

1  A  Could I have your name, please?
   B  My surname's Asada, A-S-A-D-A.
   A  And your first name, please?
   B  It's Tosh. That's T-O-S-H.

2  A  Your name please, madam?
   B  My first name's Monika.
   A  Is that M-O-N-I-C-A?
   B  No. M-O-N-I-K-A.
   A  Right. And your last name, please?
   B  Manning. M-A-double-N-I-N-G.

3 A What's your surname, please sir?
  B Gass. That's G-A-double-S.
  A And could I have your first name?
  B Karl. K-A-R-L.

4 A What is your first name please, madam?
  B Sophie. S-O-P-H-I-E. And my surname is Jacobs.
  A J-A-C-O-B-S?
  B Yes.

5 A Could I have your name please?
  B Yes, my surname's Kirkby.
  A How do you spell that?
  B Oh, it's K-I-R-K-B-Y. And my first name's Gerald. G-E-R-A-L-D.

6 A May I have your surname, please?
  B La Tuille.
  A Is that two words?
  B Yes. L-A and new word T-U-I-double-L-E.
  A And your first name?
  B Francine. F-R-A-N-C-I-N-E.

7 A What's your name please, sir?
  B Forsythe. F-O-R-S-Y-T-H-E. And my first name's Richard.
  A That's R-I-C-H-A-R-D.

8 A Could I have your name please, madam?
  B Yes, my last name's Pennington. P-E-double-N-I-N-G-T-O-N.
  A And your first name?
  B Martha. M-A-R-T-H-A

## Activity 6 (2' 50")

Listen. Did the bank clerk write down these people's names correctly? Put a tick beside their name if they are spelled correctly. Correct the names with the wrong spelling.

1 Your name's Jessie Bowman. That's J-E-S-S-I-E B-O-W-M-A-N.
2 That's Trisha Everett. T-R-I-S-H-A E-V-E-R-E-T-T.
3 And you're Seichi Shimamoto. That's S-E-I-C-H-I S-H-I-M-A-M-O-T-O.
4 And your name is spelt C-A-R-L-A M-E-S-T-A-N-Z-A.
5 Did I spell your surname correctly Miss Hazzard? That's H-A-Z-Z-A-R-D?
6 Now, your name is spelt F-E-R-N-A-N-D-O G-O-M-E-Z?
7 Could I just check your name? That's R-O-B-E-R-T C-O-H-E-N.
8 Mr Bradley Metcalfe. That's B-R-A-D-L-E-Y M-E-T-C-A-L-F-E.

## Activity 7 (1' 55")

What are these people's titles and initials? Listen and complete the guest register for a hotel.

1 A Is that Miss Agrabanti?
  B That's Doctor Agrabanti. Dr P M Agrabanti.

2 A Would that be Mrs Foster?
  B Ms Foster please. Ms K Foster.

3 A Is that Mr Corpuz?
  B Yes. Mr M P Corpuz

4 A Is that Mrs Kato?
  B Miss K Kato, please.

5 A Is that Mrs Blackburn?
  B Dr Blackburn, actually.
  A And your initials, please?
  B J D.

6 A Your initials please, Miss Chun?
  B C C.
  A It is Miss Chun, isn't it?
  B That's right.

7 A What are your initials, please?
  B D V.
  A And is that Dr Lange?
  B Mr, thank you.

8 A Is that Ms Corrigan?
  B Mrs, please.
  A And your initials Mrs Corrigan?
  B B.

# Meeting people

## Activity 1 (1' 20")

| A | | B |
|---|---|---|
| 1 | Good morning. How are you today? | Fine, thanks |
| 2 | Nice day, isn't it? | Yes, lovely. |
| 3 | How was your weekend? | Great. And yours? |
| 4 | Hi. How's everything? | Oh. OK thanks. |
| 5 | Hello. My name's Pat. | Mine's Jenny. Hello. |
| 6 | What did you say your name was? | Richard. Richard Deakin. |
| 7 | Nice to meet you. | Yes. You too. |
| 8 | How do you do? | How do you do? |
| 9 | How're you doing? | Not too bad. |
| 10 | See you later. | Yeah, OK. |
| 11 | Have a nice day. | You too. |

## Activity 2 (40")

Listen and tick the best reply to each sentence.

1 Did you say your name was Pat?
2 How have you been?
3 Nice to meet you.
4 How do you do?
5 How are things with you?
6 My name's Amir.

# Places

## Activity 1 (45")

You will hear the names of some British counties. Tick the counties you hear.

1 Berkshire    5 Lancashire
2 Cornwall    6 Tayside
3 Durham    7 Strathclyde
4 Gwent    8 West Glamorgan

## Activity 2 (1' 35")

These people are American. Where are they from? Listen and tick the correct state.

1 A You're from Pueblo, are you? That's in Colorado, not Utah, isn't it?
  B That's right.

2 A I'm from Wayne.
  B Oh. Is that in Indiana or Ohio?
  A In Indiana.

3 A So you're from Springfield. Where's that? In Iowa or Illinois?
  B Illinois!

4 A I'm from Birmingham.
  B That's in Alabama, not Georgia, isn't it?
  A Yeah.

5 A Harrisburg? That must be in Pennsylvania or West Virginia.
  B Pennsylvania, not West Virginia.

6 A Where is Prescott? New Mexico?
  B No, in Arizona.
  A Oh, of course.

7 A I'm from Great Falls. Do you know where that is?
  B I guess Montana or North Dakota.
  A Montana.

8 A I'm from Salem.
  B That's in Idaho, not Washington, isn't it?
  A Neither. It's in Oregon.

## Activity 3 (1' 10")

Where are these people living now? Listen and tick the correct city or country.

1 I've just moved from London to Manchester.
2 Oh, I'm still in Paris. I'm moving to New York next year.
3 Well, I lived in Tokyo before I moved to Hong Kong.
4 Yeah, I just moved from Dallas to St Louis.
5 I'm still living in Barcelona. I decided not to move to Madrid.
6 You know, I used to live in Italy before I moved to France.
7 I don't live in Mexico any more. I'm in Ecuador.
8 No, I've never lived in Cambridge. I've always lived here in Oxford.

## Activity 4 (1' 10")

Listen to the students in a class introduce themselves. How many students come from each of the areas below?

I'm Claude, from Hawaii.
I'm Azizah. I come from Malaysia.
My name is Celine. I come from Argentina.
I'm Alice. I'm from Tanzania.
I'm Hans, from Holland.
I'm Bashir. I come from Saudi Arabia.
I'm Marie-Hélène. I'm from Switzerland.
I'm Daeng. I come from Thailand.
I come from Kenya. My name is Said.
I'm Su, from Taiwan.

# UNIT 3

# Times

## Activity 1 (50")

five past three
twenty past seven
a quarter to two
ten past six
half past seven
twenty-five past two
twenty past four
three o' clock
five past eleven
ten to ten
ten past ten
a quarter to seven

## Activity 3 (2' 10")

Listen to people asking when the flights below arrive. Write down the arrival times using the 24 hour clock.

1 A Could you tell me when flight TW218 arrives, please?
  B Yes, it gets in at 7.45.
  A 7.45. Thanks.

2 A Has flight BA13 arrived yet?
  B No, it arrives at 15.20.

3 A Is flight AF409 coming in on time?
  B Yes, it's due in at 20.30.
  A 20.30.

4 A I'd like to know when flight LH68 gets in, please.
  B Let me check. Yes, it should arrive at 16.40.

5 A What time does flight A115 arrive?
  B Let me see. Yes, it will be here at 13.45.

6 A Can you tell me what time flight AF35 gets here?
  B Flight AF35. That should get here at 11.15.

7 A Can you tell me when flight SK70 gets in?
  B At 8.05.

8 A Do you know when flight BA502 arrives?
  B Yes, it's due in at 18.25.

## Activity 4 (1' 40")

Listen to people telephoning an office to speak to the people below. Write down the time when each person will return. It's now 10 a.m. If the operator says, 'He'll be back in an hour', write 11.00.

1 A Could I speak to Mr Day, please?
  B I'm sorry, he's not in right now. He'll be back in an hour.
  A Thanks, I'll call later.

2 A Is Ms Lewis there, please?
  B She's just gone out. She'll be back in fifteen minutes.
  A Oh, I see.

3 A Yes . . . I'd like to speak to Mr Grant, please.
  B I'm afraid he's out of the office at the moment. He won't be back for an hour.
  A Oh, I see. Well, I'll call back then.

4 A Could I speak to Mrs Ginatti, please?
  B I'm sorry, she's not here just now.
  A When will she be back, please?
  B In an hour and a half.

5 A Mr Frank, please.
  B Mr Frank's not here at the moment. But he'll be back in three quarters of an hour.
  A I see. Thank you.

6 A Is Ms Taylor there, please?
  B No, I'm sorry she isn't. She'll be back in about 40 minutes.
  A Thanks.

## Activity 5 (2' 27")

Listen to people calling the international telephone operator to ask about the time in the countries below. The caller's time is shown. Listen and write down the time in the country they ask about. For example, if the caller's time is 2 p.m. and the time in Bolivia is four hours behind, the time there is 10 a.m.

1 A I'd like to know what time it is in Bolivia, please.
  B Bolivia. Um, they're four hours behind us, so the time there is . . .

2 A Could you tell me the time right now in Haiti, please?
  B Haiti? Let me check. Yes, they're five hours behind us, so their time is. . .

3 A Yes, I want to call Finland. What time is it there now, please?
  B Well, they're two hours ahead, so the time there is . . .

4 A What time is it in Argentina now, please?
  B Argentina's three hours behind us, so the time there is . . .

5 A Do you know what time it is right now in Burma, please?

B Burma? Well, let me see. Oh, they're six and a half hours ahead of us, so their time is . . .

6 A Could you tell me what time it is in Taiwan now, please?
  B They're exactly eight hours ahead of us, so it'll be . . .

7 A What time is it in Fiji now, please?
  B Fiji. Let me see. Oh, they're twelve hours ahead of us. That means . .

8 A Could you tell me the time in Germany, please?
  B Well, Germany's one hour ahead of here, so the time there is . . .

# Dates

## Activity 1 (1' 05")

eighteen seventy-nine
nineteen fifty-two
fifteen thirty-nine
eighteen hundred
nineteen seventy-eight
seventeen sixty
nineteen thirteen
eighteen seventeen
nineteen oh one
nineteen seventy
nineteen twenty-nine
eighteen ninety-nine
nineteen oh eight
ten sixty-six

## Activity 2 (1' 38")

When did these famous writers live? Listen and write down when they were born and when they died.

1 A When did Charles Dickens live?
  B Dickens? Well, he was born in 1812 and he died in 1870.

2 A Do you know when D H Lawrence was born?
  B Yes, he was born in 1885.
  A And when did he die?
  B He died in 1930.

3 A Do you know when Jane Austen was born?
  B Yes, she lived from 1775 to 1817.
  A 1775 to 1817.
  B That's right.

4 A Is Ernest Hemingway still alive?
  B No, he died in 1961.
  A Oh. When was he born?
  B He was born in 1899.

5 A Do you know when Emily Dickinson lived?
  B Yes, she was born in 1830 and she died in 1886.

6 A When was Oscar Wilde born?
  B Oscar Wilde? Oh, in 1854.
  A And when did he die?
  B In 1900.

## Activity 3 (1' 05")

The seventh of June 1948.
The eighth of February 1985.
The twenty-third of March 1980.
The second of January 1984.
The fourteenth of November 1987.
The twenty-fourth of December 1962.
The fourth of September 1972.
The third of October 1921.
The eighth of July 1956.
The twenty-ninth of February 1980.

## Activity 4 (1' 23")

Listen to these people saying when they were born. Write down the dates. For example, if you hear,'I was born on the 28th of July, 1953', write: 28-7-53.

1  A  Could you give me the date of your birth?
   B  Oh yes, I was born on the 6th of June, 1939.
2  A  When were you born, please?
   B  I was born in 1965, on July the 6th.
3  A  I need to know your date of birth, please.
   B  It's April the 21st, 1956.
4  A  What was the date of your birth, please?
   B  1929. February the 16th.
5  A  When were you born?
   B  I was born in 1944. January the 2nd, 1944.
6  A  Could I have your date of birth, please?
   B  November the 15th, 1971.

## Activity 5 (1' 28")

When did these visitors arrive in Britain and when will they leave? Listen and circle the day each person arrived and the day they're leaving.

1  A  So, how long have you been in Britain?
   B  Well, we arrived on the 4th, and we're staying until the 20th.

2  A  Have you been here long?
   B  Just five days. We arrived on the 10th.
   A  And how long will you be here?
   B  Until the 22nd.

3  A  Have you been here long?
   B  Not long. We arrived on the fifth.
   A  Will you be staying long?
   B  Until the 19th.

4  A  So, when did you get here?
   B  Last week. On the 10th.
   A  And how long will you be here altogether?
   B  We're staying for ten days.

5  A  Have you just arrived?
   B  No, we arrived on the 6th.
   A  I see. And how long will you be staying here?
   B  We leave on the 25th.

6  A  Are you planning to stay here long?
   B  Until the 20th.
   A  I see. And when did you get here?
   B  We got here on the first of the month.

## Activity 6 (1' 30")

How long have these people been in Britain? Listen and write the number of weeks, months, or years they have been here.

1  A  How long have you been here.
   B  Let's see. I've been here for about six and a half weeks now.

2  A  Have you been living in Britain long?
   B  Yes, I came here sixteen years ago.

3  A  Have you lived here long?
   B  For about three and a half months now.

4  A  And you've been here for about three months?
   B  No, I've been here for nine months now.

5  A  So when did you first come to the UK?
   B  Oh, let me see now. Mm, it was about 26 years ago.

6  A  Did you arrive in the UK recently?
   B  Yes, I've only been here four and a half weeks.

7  A  How long have you been living in England?
   B  Mm. This is my fifth year now.

8  A  Have you been living here for very long?
   B  No, only five weeks.

## UNIT 4

# Food

### Activity 1 (48")

| | |
|---|---|
| mango | chicken |
| tuna | apple |
| cucumber | orange |
| pineapple | lobster |
| salmon | mushroom |
| turkey | grapefruit |
| onion | broccoli |
| cabbage | cauliflower |

### Activity 2 (48")

You will hear sentences containing the phrase a or the. Listen and tick the one you hear.

1  Could you pass me the cauliflower?
2  Did you buy a grapefruit?
3  Would you cut up the cabbage, please?
4  Is that a salmon?
5  How much is a lobster?
6  Do you need the pineapple?
7  Please cut up a cucumber for me.

### Activity 3 (52")

Tim is going to the supermarket. Listen and tick the things he needs to buy.

1 I'd better get some broccoli today.
2 I don't think I need to get any more cabbage.
3 I ought to get some rice, I suppose.
4 I won't need to get any sweetcorn this week.
5 We certainly need some more onions.
6 We do need some more bread.
7 We've still got plenty of cucumber.
8 I'll try to find some fresh lamb.

# Recipes

### Activity 1 (1' 55")

You will hear the ingredients for three recipes. Listen and write down the amounts needed.

1 A Now you'll need about 800 grams of beef.
  B OK.
  A Then 250 grams of chopped onions.
  B Yes, and how much tomato purée?
  A About three tablespoons is enough. Then you'll need some curry powder. I use about one and a half tablespoons.
  B Fine. What about salt and pepper?
  A Use about half a teaspoon of salt and about a quarter of a teaspoon of pepper.

2 A How many eggs do I need?
  B About half a dozen.
  A Fine. And then what?
  B About 200 grams of sliced onions. And about 250 grams of mushrooms.
  A 200 grams of sliced onions and 250 grams of mushrooms.
  B Yes. And half a litre of cream.
  A Mmm.
  B Half a teaspoon of salt and half a teaspoon of pepper.
  A Yes. And what about the cheese?
  B Oh, yes. It takes about 175 grams of cheese.

3 A Now start with about a kilo of chicken.
  B Yes.
  A And about 250 grams of small onions.
  B Fine. What next?
  A Then you'll need about 150 grams of chopped bacon.
  B About 150 grams.
  A Then about a quarter of a litre of red wine.
  B A quarter of a litre. And how much flour?
  A You'll need about 75 grams.

# In a restaurant

### Activity 1 (1' 30")

You will hear a waiter taking people's orders in a restaurant. Listen and tick their orders.

1 A Have you decided on your order?
  B Yes, I'll have the chicken, please.
  A And would you like rice or potatoes with that?
  B Potatoes, please.
  A Would you like vegetables as well?
  B I don't think so, thanks.
  A And what would you like to drink?
  B I'll have orange juice, please.

2 A Can I take your order?
  B I think I'll try the beef. I'd like that rare, please.
  A Certainly. Would you like rice or potatoes with it?
  B Mm. Rice, please. And I'll have vegetables, as well.
  A Anything to drink?
  B Coffee, please.

3 A What would you like to have?
  B I think I'll try the fish.
  A With rice?
  B Yes, please.
  A Will you have vegetables?
  B Yes, please.
  A And to drink?
  B Nothing, thank you.

### Activity 2 (1' 18")

Listen to people talking about their meals. Did they enjoy their food? Tick the correct response for each speaker.

1 A How was it?
  B Mm. Very nice.

2 A Did you enjoy your meal?
  B It was all right.

3 A How was your fish?
  B Not very good, I'm afraid.

4 A This steak is terrible.
  B Really?

5 A How are the vegetables?
  B Delicious.

6 A Is the soup nice?
  B Not bad.

### Activity 3 (57")

Listen to people talking about their food. What do they mean? Tick the correct explanation.

1 Could you heat this up for me?
2 This has been cooked too long.
3 This is tasteless. It needs more salt.
4 This meat is awful. I can't even chew it.
5 This needs cooking a little longer.
6 This is too hot for me, I'm afraid.
7 I asked for coffee without sugar.

## Activity 4 (45")

Listen to the waitress and choose the best response.

1  Is everything OK?
2  How's your meal?
3  Would you like anything to drink?
4  Can I get you some more coffee?
5  How much sauce would you like?
6  Is the steak all right?
7  Can I get you anything else?

# U N I T 5

# Furniture and rooms

## Activity 2 (57")

You will hear eight of the words from the list above. Number the words you hear from 1 - 8, and underline the stressed syllable.

a cooker
a shower
a fireplace
a washing machine
a wardrobe
a stereo system
a bookcase
a television

## Activity 3 (1' 10")

Rita wants to rent a flat. You will hear her talking to a landlord about it. Which room is the landlord describing? Choose a or b.

1  A  And what's the living room like?
   B  Quite big. It's got a sofa and two chairs as well as a dining table.

2  A  Is there a shower as well as a bath in the bathroom?
   B  No, there's only a shower, I'm afraid.

3  A  What's the bedroom got in it?
   B  A double bed and a dressing table.

4  A  Could you tell me about the kitchen?
   B  Well, it's got a new cooker and a small fridge, and plenty of cupboards.

5  A  What's the small bedroom got in it?
   B  Just a bed and a small chest of drawers.

## Activity 4 (55")

Mrs Keane has just arrived at her hotel. Listen to the porter showing her where things are in her room. Number the correct places in the picture.

This is your room Mrs Keane. I hope you'll be comfortable here. You'll find your towels in the bathroom. The light switch for the bathroom is to the right of the door. The phone's next to your bed and there's a phone book in the drawer underneath. If you'd like some coffee or tea there's a kettle and a cup and saucer on the shelf above the desk. On the desk you'll find some information about the hotel. There's an ashtray next to the phone on the bedside table.

## Activity 5 (1' 28")

Listen to people talking about where they live. Tick the picture of the house or building they are talking about.

1  A  What's your new house like Jean?
   B  It's nice. It's got a big garage, which is what I like.

2  A  Is your house that stone one with the fence around it?
   B  Yes, that's right.

3  A  Do you still live in that lovely old house on Elm Street?
   B  Yes. It's the one with the big trees around it.

4  A  Have you got a garden?
   B  No, we haven't, unfortunately.

5  A  What's your block of flats like?
   B  It's an old four-storey building.

6  A  Which floor is your flat on?
   B  I live on the top floor.

7  A  Where's the entrance to your block of flats?
   B  It's at the side.

8  A  Can you park near your flat?
   B  Yes, there are several parking spaces in front of the building.

# At home

## Activity 1 (1' 15")

Listen to people phoning their friends. Tick where each person is.

1  A  Could I speak to Kathy, please?
   B  Do you want me to get her? She's working on her car.

2  A  Is Bill there, please?
   B  Yes, just a moment. I think he's still asleep.

3  A  I'd like to speak to Susan, please.
   B  Could you ring back in ten minutes? She's just having a bath.

4  A  Is Terry there, please?
   B  Oh, he's not here right now.

5  A  Could I speak to Mr Lee, please?
   B  Could you call back in a little while. He's cooking right now.

6  A  Is Helen busy at the moment?
   B  Well she's just watching the volley-ball game on television. I'll get her.

## Activity 2 (1')

Roy and Sylvia have a lot of things to do this weekend. Listen to them deciding which things they want to do. Put a tick in the correct column to show who does what. The first one has been done for you.

**Sylvia** There's so much to do today. What do you want to do?

**Roy** Well, I'll clean the bathroom, if you like.

**Sylvia** OK, and I'll take out the rubbish. What about the shopping?

**Roy** Oh, I'll go shopping. I tell you what, I'll clean the car and then go shopping.

**Sylvia** Right. I'll vacuum the carpet, then. But I need to clean the fridge.

**Roy** Oh, leave the fridge. Clean it next week.

**Sylvia** OK, but I'll clean the windows.

**Roy** All right, and I'll put the groceries away when I get back.

**Sylvia** Fine. I'm going to leave the sheets. I'll iron them later.

## Activity 3 (45")

You are at home with your flatmate Virginia. Listen to what she says. What do you think she is going to ask you to do? Tick what you think she will ask.

1   I'd like to watch the news.
2   I'm getting rather hungry.
3   It's very windy outside.
4   It's very dark in here.
5   It's very cold in this room.

# UNIT 6

# Prices

There are three ways of saying prices and amounts of money in English. Eight point five oh can be said eight pounds and fifty pence; eight pounds fifty and eight fifty. In this unit you will hear all three ways. This will help you to learn and recognize them.

## Activity 1 (1' 45")

sixteen pounds fifty
sixty pounds and five pence
fourteen ninety-five
forty pounds nineteen
twenty-two seventy
eighteen thirty-five
ninety-three pounds and four pence
two hundred and nine pounds and sixty-four pence
three hundred and fifty pounds fifty-five
six hundred and twenty pounds thirty pence
thirty-five thousand six hundred and thirty-seven pounds
sixty-six thousand and nineteen pounds
one hundred and forty-nine thousand five hundred and ninety pounds
one million and one hundred pounds

## Activity 2 (1' 27")

Listen and tick the prices you hear.

1   That's fifty-six fifty altogether.
2   That comes to eleven seventeen.
3   The total is sixty-nine pounds nine pence.
4   It costs one thousand and sixty-seven pounds.
5   That comes to a hundred and nine pounds and forty-five pence.
6   The price is one hundred and ninety-eight thousand pounds.
7   That's five hundred and fifty pounds.
8   They cost fifteen thousand six hundred and seventy pounds.
9   It was sold for one hundred and seventy-five thousand, nine hundred pounds.
10   They sold it for one million, three hundred and fifty thousand pounds.

## Activity 3 (1' 15")

Listen to the cashier add up these restaurant bills. Did he enter the correct prices? Put a tick or cross in each box.

1   Now that's eleven fifty for the main course, one twenty-five for the salad. The drinks were two pounds thirty and the dessert one ninety.
2   Your starters were five pounds sixty, and the main courses twenty seventy; drinks were six fifteen and the desserts cost four pounds and five pence.
3   Your main course was five seventy-five, the salad was one fifty, drinks were three pounds ninety and the dessert was two thirty-five.
4   The main courses came to fourteen pounds fifty, the salads were three pounds and the drinks two eighty.

## Activity 4 (2' 03")

Listen to a customs officer at Heathrow Airport asking David Carter how much he paid for the things he bought on holiday. Write the correct price next to each item and what its value is in pounds.

**Co** Excuse me sir, can I ask you where you've just travelled from?

**David** Yes, from Hong Kong. And I've been to Tokyo and Singapore too.

**Co** Is this your luggage? Can I look in your bag? (pause)
Did you buy these things on holiday?

**David** Yes, I did.

**Co** How much did you pay for the watch?

**David** Oh, let me see, I've got the receipts here. Yes, that was a hundred and forty Hong Kong dollars.

**Co** One hundred and forty Hong Kong dollars. Right, that's about ten pounds. And the calculator?

**David** Oh, that was only, er, thirty-five dollars in Hong Kong.

**Co** Thirty-five dollars. Erm, that's about two pounds fifty. What did this cassette recorder cost?

**David** The cassette recorder? That cost eleven thousand three hundred and sixty yen. I bought it in Tokyo.

**Co** Eleven thousand three hundred and sixty yen - that must be about fifty pounds. Did you buy this necklace while you were away?

**David** Yes I did, in Singapore. It cost ninety-one dollars.

**Co** Right, that's about, twenty-five pounds. So, ten pounds for the watch, two fifty for the calculator, fifty pounds for the cassette recorder and twenty-five pounds for the necklace. Right, so you spent more than eighty-seven pounds. Did you know that thirty two pounds is the most you can spend tax-free?

## Activity 5 (1' 55")

Listen to the people comparing the prices of things in three different cities. Listen and list the cities from the most expensive (1) to the least expensive (3).

1 A loaf of bread costs under a pound in London; it's cheaper in Paris, around fifty pence, and only costs thirty-five pence in Madrid.

2 A cinema ticket costs around five pounds in New York; in London you pay about four pounds and in Tokyo it's about six pounds fifty.

3 A one mile taxi ride in Singapore costs about one pound fifty; in Tokyo it comes to about five pounds, and in Honolulu you pay about three pounds.

4 A good meal at a first class restaurant costs about forty dollars in Chicago, about forty-five dollars in San Francisco, and about thirty dollars in Phoenix.

5 A flat of about a thousand square feet costs about two hundred pounds a week to rent in Mexico City; about two hundred and fifty pounds a week in Los Angeles and about a hundred and fifty pounds a week in Hong Kong.

6 Posting a local letter costs around eight pence in Rio, twelve pence in Washington and about fifteen pence in Jakarta.

# Paying

## Activity 1 (1' 15")

Listen to people paying for things in a department store. How do they pay for each item? Tick the correct box.

1 A How would you like to pay for this?
  B Can I pay by cheque?
  A Yes. Have you got a cheque card?
  B Yes, I have.

2 A Can I pay by credit card?
  B Yes, we take Barclaycard, Access and American Express.
  A Fine, I'll use Barclaycard.

3 A Do you want to pay by credit card, Sir?
  B I'll use a traveller's cheque, please.
  A I'm sorry, we don't take traveller's cheques.
  B Then I'll pay cash. You do take that, don't you?

4 A How will you pay for this, please?
  B I'll pay by Access. Here's my card.

## Activity 2 (1' 55")

Listen to people changing traveller's cheques at a bank. How much money do they want to change? How many of each kind of note do they want?

1 A I'd like to change these traveller's cheques, please.
  B Certainly, how much would you like to change?
  A Three hundred and fifty, please.
  B And how would you like that?
  A In fifties, please.

2 A Could I change these traveller's cheques, please?
  B Yes. How many have you got there?
  A Five hundred pounds.
  B Right, just sign them, please. And how would you like that?
  A I'd like ten twenties, three fifties, and the rest in tens.

3 A Can I help you?
  B Yes, I'd like to change these cheques.
  A Yes. How many, please?
  B I've got fifteen hundred pounds worth.
  A Certainly. Just sign them for me. And how would you like that?
  B In large notes, please. Could I have twenty fifties and the rest in twenties please.

4 A Would you like to change those?
  B Yes, please.
  A How much do you have?
  B A hundred and fifty altogether.
  A And how would you like it?
  B In tens and twenties, please.
  A Shall I give you five twenties and the rest in tens?
  B Yes, that's fine.

## Activity 3 (1' 52")

Listen to people thinking about buying the things below. Will they buy the item, buy something else, or not buy anything? Tick what you think they will do.

1 I'd really love to buy that sofa. But £600 is much more than I want to spend. Well, perhaps I'll get the chairs instead.

2 It's time I got a new television. This one is £150. That's not too bad. I thought it would be more.

3 This new fridge is really nice. It's got lots of room. But it's nearly four hundred pounds. I really don't think I need a new one yet.

4 I like this car. Let me see. If I put down a deposit of £500 then it'll cost me about £150 a month. Yes, that's not too bad. I can afford that.

5 Oh, that dress is fabulous! I can just see myself in it. But £200 - no way!

6 This coat would be very useful in the winter, but I've got a good raincoat and I need a new suit.

### Activity 4 (1' 05")

Listen to these questions about money and prices and choose the best response.

1 How much is the camera?
2 Do you have anything cheaper?
3 Did you say £1510?
4 How much money do you want to spend?
5 Which is the cheaper, the ring or the bracelet?
6 The meal was really good. How much shall we tip the waitress?
7 I'm sorry, I made a mistake with your bill.
8 Sorry, you made a mistake with the bill.

# UNIT 7

# Health

### Activity 2 (1' 10")

You will hear sentences containing one of the words in each pair below. Circle the word you hear.

1 Yes, my nose is very sore. I think I'll get something from the chemist for it.
2 I've got a really stiff neck today.
3 The pain is just here, by my hips.
4 I use this oil on my hair.
5 My throat is much better today.
6 Let me just check your wrist.
7 Use this cream on your ears.
8 I've got a pain in the back of my leg.

### Activity 3 (1' 09")

You will hear people describing where they feel pain. Which part of the body are they describing? Number the parts described.

1 The pain is here on the top of my shoulder.
2 It hurts here, just above my nose.
3 It's my big toe which hurts.
4 It's this lower tooth which is painful.
5 It hurts here at the back of my neck.
6 Yes, my knee is quite sore.
7 When I stand my ankle hurts.
8 I've got an awful pain in my stomach.

### Activity 4 (1' 35")

Listen to these people describing how they feel. Number the sentences from 1 - 8 according to what's wrong with them.

1 Yes, I feel quite awful. I feel hot and tired, and my nose is running. I have to blow my nose every five minutes.
2 My head feels dreadful. Every few minutes I get a strong, sharp pain.

3 If I don't move my head it's all right, but when I try to turn my head I feel this terrible pain.
4 I got it caught in the car door. It's really painful. I can't write either.
5 I can't eat anything. It really hurts when I chew on it. I must go and see the dentist.
6 When I try to walk on it, it hurts a lot.
7 It's very painful. I can't swallow food very easily and it hurts when I cough.
8 No, it's just my left one that hurts. And I can't hear at all well with it.

### Activity 5 (1' 14")

Listen to the doctor telling people what medicine to take. Write out what they have to take and how often each day.

1 Now, I want you to take a teaspoon of this medicine in the morning and another in the afternoon . . .
2 You must take two tablets three times a day.
3 Just take one tablet in the morning. Don't take another one until the next day.
4 Take a teaspoon and a half of this medicine six times a day.
5 Take two tablets with a glass of water every twelve hours.
6 Take three teaspoonfuls three times a day.
7 Take two tablets when you get up in the morning and another two before you go to bed at night.

### Activity 6 (1' 32")

How did these people hurt themselves? Listen and number the pictures 1-8.

1 Yes, I was at the top of the ladder trying to put away the dishes when I slipped and fell.
2 Well, I hurt my arm as I was climbing out of the pool after a swim.
3 I was running along the side of the road when I tripped and hurt my ankle.
4 I was hurrying out of the office to get to my car when someone opened a door and I ran straight into it.
5 I was making a cup of coffee when I spilt boiling water over my hand.
6 I was just coming out of the sea after a swim when I stepped on a sharp stone and cut my foot.
7 Suddenly a car pulled out and I couldn't stop in time and rode straight into it.
8 It had been raining and the ground was wet. That's how I slipped. Next time I won't play on a wet tennis court.

### Activity 7 (1')

Listen to people talking about how they feel. Tick the best response.

1 Yes, my headache's nearly gone. I feel much better now.
2 I think I'm getting a cold.
3 Poor John! He broke his arm last weekend.
4 This headache's really killing me. It's awful.

5   I have to go to the doctor.
6   My ear's much better today.
7   My tooth is really painful.

# Exercise

## Activity 1 (1' 10")

How do these people keep fit? Listen and tick what they say.

1   Well, I go to the pool at least three times a week. It really keeps me fit.
2   I play tennis about twice a week in the summer. Then, in the winter I play basketball.
3   I like to take long walks. And I walk to work whenever I can.
4   I cycle. I often ride twenty miles or so. I love it.
5   I belong to a gym. I go there for a good workout twice a week.
6   I'm a jogger. I run every day after work for an hour.
7   I exercise at home every day. I don't like playing sports very much.

# UNIT 8

# Describing objects

## Activity 2 (43")

Listen and circle the words you hear.

| | | | |
|---|---|---|---|
| 1 | radios | 5 | watch |
| 2 | shoe | 6 | suitcases |
| 3 | glass | 7 | umbrella |
| 4 | brushes | 8 | bottles |

## Activity 3 (1' 20")

You will hear people talking about seven of the things in the pictures below. Number them from 1 - 7.

1   Yes, it's very comfortable and wide enough for three people to sit on.
2   There's plenty of room inside for your clothes. It's big enough to take everything you need when you're going on holiday.
3   These are very comfortable to wear and they're wonderful when you're playing tennis.
4   It's quite light and easy to carry. You can carry it home from the office if you want to do some typing at home.
5   There's room for two people in front and three in the back.
6   It's small, but you can get a packed lunch and an extra jumper in it.
7   It's made of wood, so it's quite light. You can eat off it when you're watching television, too.

## Activity 4 (1' 08")

You will hear people at a lost property office describing things they have lost. Circle a, b or c to identify the correct item for each person.

1   It's a small suitcase with a strap round it.
2   It's got a round neck and long sleeves.
3   It's a big square parcel tied with string.
4   It's made of real leather. It hasn't got a strap.
5   It's a white beach hat with a dark band.
6   It's got two pockets on the front and buttons.
7   It's got a checked pattern on it.

## Activity 5 (1' 36")

Listen to people returning things to a department store. What's wrong with each item? Tick the best answer.

1   I'm afraid I'll have to change these shoes. I just can't get into them. Have you got a bigger size?
2   I'd like a sweater with longer sleeves. These are too short.
3   There's something wrong with this clock. It gains about an hour every day.
4   I'm afraid there isn't a key for the lock on this bag.
5   I can't hear any sound on these earphones.
6   I can't get this umbrella to open properly. It seems to get stuck.
7   I can't get this torch to work. I don't think there's anything wrong with the battery.

# Describing people

## Activity 1 (1' 33")

You will hear people describing someone they are looking for at a party. Listen and number the people correctly from 1 - 7.

1   Do you know where Sandra is? She's the one in jeans with short curly hair.
2   Have you seen my friend Doug? He's wearing a dark suit and a tie.
3   I'm looking for Stephen. He's the bald man with the moustache.
4   Do you know where Mike is? He's the big man with glasses.
5   Have you seen Monica? She's the one in dark glasses and trousers.
6   I'm looking for Paul. He's the one in shorts.
7   Can you see Jenny anywhere? She's wearing quite a long skirt.

## Activity 2 (1' 16")

You will hear people talking about their families. Listen and write the correct name under each member of the families.

1   Well, that's my older sister Tracy, the one in glasses. And this is Jenny in the dark sweater on her left. That's my brother Paul in the striped shirt, and the one next to Jenny is my brother Kevin.

2   This is my father in the checked shirt on the left. And that's my brother David on the right in the T-shirt. The one with the striped blouse is my sister Ellen. Oh, this is Karen in the jacket. And the other one is me.

3   The tall girl is my sister Susan. The short lad is my brother Dick. That's my older brother, Fred, in the sweater, and the other one is my sister Margaret.

## Activity 3 (1' 20")

You will hear sentences about different people. If the sentence sounds like this:

She's wearing a green blouse.

the speaker is making a statement. If the sentence sounds like this:

She's wearing a green blouse?

the speaker is asking a question. Listen and tick under statement or question.

1   That's your sister Eileen.
2   Bill's the one wearing a jacket?
3   Richard's your older brother?
4   My brother's a student.
5   Brian's Ellen's brother?
6   David's the one in glasses.
7   Fred's the one in the suit?
8   Frank's the one wearing jeans.

# UNIT 9

# Shops and shopping

## Activity 1 (35")

paperback
weekend groceries
frying pan
ladder
garden tools
coffee table
tennis shoes
photography magazine
newspaper

## Activity 2 (38")

Shirley and Roger are talking about the things they've got to do when they're out. Tick the places they'll go to on the list below.

A   Well, the first thing we should do is post these letters.
B   Yes. Then after that, I'd like to buy some shelves for the living room.
A   That's a good idea, but we musn't forget to get some cat food for Sandy. There's only one tin left.
B   And I think I'd like to buy a nice cake for the weekend.

## Activity 3 (1' 26")

Roger's going to the supermarket. He's checking the things below in the kitchen. Listen and decide whether there's a lot, a little, or none at all. Tick the correct box.

1   Mm. We've only got two slices of bread left. I'd better get some more.
2   There seems to be a whole packet of butter, so I won't need to get any more.
3   We've run out of milk. I'd better get some.
4   We still have two boxes of eggs, so I won't get any.
5   We've got about half a pound of sugar - that should be enough for the rest of the week, but I'll get some anyway.
6   Now vegetables . . . Um. We've only got a couple of tomatoes and a few beans. I'll get some more.
7   I've got a full bottle of cooking oil. I won't get any more.
8   The ketchup is finished. I'd better get a new bottle.

## Activity 4 (1' 58")

Shirley and Roger are deciding where to buy some of the things they need. They'll go to one of the places below. Listen and tick the name of the shop they're going to.

1   A   We could get the meat at Ace or Star Supermarket.
    B   Let's got to Ace. It's difficult to get a parking space at Star.

2   A   Where shall we go for the bread?
    B   West's and King's are both very good. But I think the bread's fresher at West's, so let's go there.

3   A   Where do you want to get the flowers?
    B   There's always a better choice at Regal, but the staff are always so rude. I don't want to shop there again.

4   A   We'll have to get some paint. I see there's a sale on at Crest.
    B   Ted's have also got a sale on this week, as well.
    A   But there's more choice at Crest, so let's go there.

5   A   I want a couple of books. Shall we go to the University Bookshop?
    B   Yes, good idea. They're not usually as expensive as Hill's Bookshop.

6   A   Do you want to get your shoes at Ellis's or Liberty's?
    B   Well, I'd like to go to Liberty's but I don't think they're open today.
    A   Oh well, we can try Ellis's.

7   A   And we'd better get some vegetables.
    B   Yes, but let's not go to Hollins. Their vegetables are never very fresh.

Now listen again. Why did they decide to go to the shops they chose? Tick the reason below.

## Activity 5 (2' 21")

Some of the items below are for sale in a newspaper. Listen to people phoning to ask questions about them. Number the eight things talked about from 1 - 8.

1   A   And is it colour or black and white?
    B   It's colour.
    A   What size is it?
    B   It's nineteen inches.
    A   And how old is it?
    B   It's only six months old.

2   A   Is it a single or a double?
    B   It's a single.
    A   And it's quite new, isn't it?
    B   Yes, it was brand new when I bought it two weeks ago.

3   A   How many miles has it done?
    B   Fifty thousand.
    A   Is it a two or four-door?
    B   It's got four doors.
    A   And how long have you had it?
    B   Six years.

4   A   Has it got any drawers?
    B   Yes, it's got two drawers in the front.
    A   And it's only three months old?
    B   That's right.

5   A   How big is it?
    B   It's about a metre and a half tall and seventy centimetres wide.
    A   And the freezer is at the top?
    B   That's right.
    A   How long have you had it?
    B   For five years.

6   A   Has it got a flash?
    B   Yes. And it's also got a cover.
    A   How long have you had it?
    B   Only nine months.

7   A   What about a dryer?
    B   Yes, it's a dryer as well.
    A   And how old is it?
    B   We bought it last year, so it's almost a year old now.

8   A   My son loves fish, so it would be good. How big is it?
    B   It's seventy centimetres wide, forty centimetres high, and thirty centimetres deep.
    A   And have you had it for long?
    B   No, we only bought it last month.

Now listen again. How old is each thing? Tick the correct box.

## Activity 6 (1' 45")

Listen to people asking where places are in a department store. Mark each of these places.

1   A   I'm looking for the toy section, please.
    B   It's in the middle of the shop, in front of the escalator.

2   A   Where's the magazine section?
    B   The magazines are at the back of the shop, in the corner on the left.

3   A   Where's the sports department, please?
    B   Near the back of the shop, in front of the till.

4   A   Could you tell me where the menswear section is?
    B   Yes, it's down on the left near the back of the shop, opposite the jewellery section.

5   A   Where are the women's clothes please?
    B   About half way down on the right, opposite the escalator.

6   A   Where can I find the kitchenware, please?
    B   Go to the back of the store. It's in the right hand corner.

7   A   I'm looking for the cosmetics counters.
    B   They're down here on the left, just before you get to the plant section.

## Activity 7 (2' 20")

You will hear people buying presents. Listen and decide what you think they will buy. Tick the correct item.

1   Well, I gave her a record last year. This year I'd better get something different. Er. Perhaps some perfume because she doesn't really like jewellery.
2   I think he'd like some clothes. Perhaps a sweater, a scarf maybe, or some socks? Could I see the sweater, please? I don't think the socks or the scarf are the right colour.
3   This red blouse is nice. The yellow one's too bright I think, and the green one isn't as pretty.
4   Yes, he loves toys. The tank's quite fun. And this little car's nice, and so's this red lorry. But I think I like the lorry best.
5   The vase is pretty but it's very expensive. Oh, this dish is nice . . . but I think I like the plate better.
6   I'm sure she'd like this necklace. The bracelet's lovely and so are the ear-rings, but I don't think she wears bracelets or ear-rings very often.
7   Well, I don't want to get anything very expensive. The soap's only £4. The aftershave's £8. That's too much. And the cologne's £15. No, I don't think I want to spend more than £5.

# UNIT 10

# Going on holiday

## Activity 2 (1' 12")

Listen to these people on holiday planning what they're going to do. Number what you hear from 1 - 5.

1  Well, the bus will pick us up at nine o'clock. The tour lasts about four hours, so we should be back at about one o' clock.
2  There's a show at eight p.m. and then the late show is at eleven p.m. Let's go to the late show.
3  The seafood here is supposed to be really good. Let's try it, shall we? I'm really hungry.
4  It says in the guide book they've got a lot of famous paintings. Let's go and have a look. It's free, too.
5  The prices here are supposed to be quite good. I really need some new clothes and some shoes . . . Let's go and see what we can find.

## Activity 3 (1' 32")

Listen to people talking about their holidays. What places did they visit? Tick the places they visited in each list below.

1  We really loved Japan. We wanted to go to Korea, too, but there wasn't time. Then we went on to Hong Kong. I love Chinese cities. We finished with a week in Thailand. It was all very exciting.
2  Well, we started in Holland, but decided not to go to France. So we went to Spain instead. It's a beautiful country. We didn't go to Italy this year, but went straight on to Greece.
3  I'm sorry we went to Los Angeles. It's an ugly place. But we loved San Francisco. Then we went on to Boston. We had to change planes in Chicago. We had a couple of days in Boston and New York, and then found we didn't have time to go to Washington.
4  We started in Paris and drove up to Brussels. Then we flew to Munich for a week. We were going to stop in Vienna, but we didn't have time,  so we went on to Rome. Some friends came up from Naples to join us.

## Activity 4 (1' 37")

Listen to people talking about different cities. What can you do in each place? Tick the lists below.

1  It's not really the best place to shop. Prices are too high there nowadays. But the food's great and quite cheap. It's a wonderful place just to walk around in and look at the old buildings. But there aren't any interesting  museums or art galleries, I'm afraid.
2  It's a very nice place to visit if you like being outdoors. The scenery is beautiful. Take a bus trip around the island, and sail around it if you have time. You can also go skiing. Unfortunately, the water is too cold there for swimming. You probably won't like the local food. It's very spicy.
3  There are very good beaches there. Everything's quite cheap, so take plenty of money with you! There's not much else to do. There's only  one hotel and no interesting old buildings.
4  There are several excellent museums and art galleries. If you like Chinese food you should visit Chinatown. It's fairly quiet at night though. It doesn't have any good nightclubs or theatres.

## Activity 5 (1' 30")

Listen to people getting ready for their holidays. Tick the things they're going to take with them.

1  I'm not going to take many things with me this time, so I won't need the big suitcase. Let's see. I think we can buy presents for our friends when we get there. They'll have music on the plane, so I won't need my personal stereo, but I'd better take something to read. It'll be fairly cool at this time of the year, so I don't suppose we'll be doing any swimming. I'd better pack the umbrella in case it rains. I'll need a thick coat, too, if it's going to be cold. That's about everything.
2  I'll put all our things into the big suitcase. Now, where are those presents we bought? I'll put them in the top. I think I'll get a new camera as soon as I arrive. I won't take my old one. You might want to listen to music on the plane, so I'll take the personal stereo. I won't take these books, they're too heavy. The weather should be good at this time of the year, so we'll be able to do some swimming. We won't need coats or umbrellas. I'll put in some air-sickness tablets in case we need them.

## Activity 6 (1' 42")

Listen to people talking about their holidays. Did they enjoy themselves? Tick the best answer.

1  The people were very friendly and the hotel was great. It was a really wonderful holiday.
2  Well, the food was good but the prices were terrible. And the hotel wasn't very quiet.
3  The beaches are beautiful but the cities are very dirty. And don't travel on the local buses, they're awful!
4  Everyone was so rude, and the food wasn't very good. We'll certainly never go there again.
5  The temperature was just right. We both like hot weather. The hotel was very cheap too, and the local food is delicious.
6  Oh, the scenery's beautiful, lovely lakes and mountains. And prices are much better than here. It's a pity the weather was so bad while we were there, though.
7  I enjoyed the shopping best of all. The department stores are great. The hotels, of course, are very clean and modern and the staff are so helpful.

## Activity 7 (55")

Listen to questions about travel and choose the best answer.

1  How did you enjoy your trip?
2  Have you been here long?
3  How long are you going to be here?
4  Where did you go for your holiday?
5  When did you get back from Japan?
6  Have you ever been to Australia?
7  How long were you away?
8  What did you think of Wales?

# UNIT 11

# Transport

## Activity 2 (1' 08")

You will hear sentences containing one of the phrases below. Tick the phrase you hear.

1  I'll be riding a blue moped.
2  I've just bought myself a gold sports car.
3  I'll be driving a bright blue van.
4  The one you want is a green bus.
5  There it is, coming in now. The green plane.
6  Try to get the fast train.
7  I'll be in a dark brown Mini.
8  She drives a light blue Toyota.

## Activity 3 (1' 08")

You will hear people describing their transport. Tick the correct box, a or b.

1  I've got one of those big old American cars. It's huge.
2  I've just bought a moped. But I can't use it at night because it doesn't have any lights.
3  I've got a new Japanese car. It's a two-door model.
4  Our van's great. I like the sliding doors. It's so easy to get in and out of.
5  I've just bought a sports car. The top folds right back. It's really fun.
6  I ride a bicycle. Unfortunately, it's not one of those light modern bicycles, but a really old one.

## Activity 4 (1' 50")

You will hear people asking about buses from the bus station to the places below. What number bus or buses can they take and how often do the buses go? If a bus goes every 20 minutes, write 20 mins under 'frequency'

1  A  What bus can I take to get to the zoo, please?
   B  Either a 17 or a 24.
   A  And how often do they leave?
   B  Every 20 minutes.

2  A  What number is the airport bus, please?
   B  That's a number 25.

   A  Does it go very often?
   B  Every five minutes.

3  A  I want to get a bus to the museum, please.
   B  Yes, you can take a number 44 or a number 50.
   A  How often do they leave?
   B  Every half hour.

4  A  What bus will take me to the university, please?
   B  The university? That would be number 16 or number 22.
   A  And do they leave often?
   B  Yes, every 20 minutes.

5  A  Can I take a bus to the hospital from here?
   B  Yes, you want a number 65.
   A  And when does it leave, please?
   B  There's one every 45 minutes.

6  A  What bus should I take to go to the public library?
   B  Number 13. It leaves every quarter of an hour.

## Activity 5 (1' 28")

You will hear people talking to a taxi driver. Where does each passenger want to go? Number the places 1-6.

1  Oh, I hope we won't arrive late. My flight leaves in half an hour.
2  Yes, we're having dinner there with friends. I hear the food is very good.
3  Can you drive a little faster, please? My class starts in ten minutes. I don't want to be late or the professor gets very angry.
4  It starts at 7.30, so there's plenty of time, and we've already got the tickets.
5  Please drive as quickly as you can. My appointment with the doctor is for 10.45.
6  I haven't been there before. I believe they've got some very good French paintings.

# Street directions

## Activity 1 (2' 20")

You will hear visitors in a city asking where places are. Listen and circle the place which is closer to the speakers.

1  A  Is the Bank of Scotland in this street?
   B  Yes, it's about two hundred yards further on.
   A  And how about the Clydesdale?
   B  That's quite a long walk the other way.

2  A  How far is the Star Supermarket from here?
   B  Let's see. It's about half a mile.
   A  And what about the Everfresh?
   B  That's just a little way down the street.

3  A  Is the Palace Restaurant far away?
   B  No, keep going for about two hundred yards.
   A  And what about the Hong Kong Restaurant?
   B  You've just passed it. It's about half a minute's walk from here.

4   A   Where's the Royal Hotel, please?
    B   It's on the other side of town. It's about five miles from here.
    A   And what about the Rose Hotel?
    B   That's about twenty minutes walk from here.

5   A   How can I get to the Natural History Museum?
    B   Take a taxi. It's about two miles from here.
    A   And what about the Museum of Modern Art?
    B   It's in the street parallel to this one, about two minutes away.

6   A   I'm looking for Mediterranean Travel.
    B   You're a long way away. It's at the very end of North Street.
    A   I see. And what about National Travel?
    B   Oh that's even further. It's out by the railway station.

## Activity 2 (1' 30")

You will hear people asking where the places below are. Number the correct places on the map.

1   A   Where's the nearest chemist, please?
    B   It's on the corner of West Street and Cross Street.

2   A   Is there a post office near here?
    B   Yes, in Newman Street, next to the art gallery.

3   A   Excuse me, where can I find a bookshop?
    B   There's one on the corner of Cross Street and Newman Street.

4   A   Could you tell me where the supermarket is, please?
    B   Yes, in West Street, between the cinema and the hotel.

5   A   I'm looking for a petrol station.
    B   There's one opposite the art gallery, in Newman Street.

6   A   Is there a bus stop near here?
    B   Yes, in front of the church in Newman Street.

## Activity 3 (2' 05")

Listen to people being given directions to the places below. Mark the directions on the map and write in the correct letter for the places they're looking for.

1   A   I'm looking for the Star Hotel.
    B   Oh, yes. Go along Bell Lane until you come to the bridge. Cross over the bridge and it's on your left.

2   A   Is there a bank near here?
    B   Go down to the end of Pine Street and turn right into Harris Street. The bank's on the right.

3   A   I'm looking for a hairdresser.
    B   Let me think. Oh, yes. I know where there's one. Go down Bell Lane and turn left into Oak Avenue. You'll find one on the corner of Oak Avenue and Harris Street.

4   A   Where's the nearest supermarket, please?
    B   Just a second. Go down Pine Street and turn into Hopper Road. Walk right to the end, and you'll see one on your right.

5   A   Can you tell me where I can find a travel agent?
    B   Certainly. Go down Bell Lane, cross the bridge, and there's one on your right, opposite the hotel.

6   A   I'm looking for a dry cleaner.
    B   Um, let's see. Go down Pine Street and turn into Harris Street. You'll see one on the left, just past the corner.

# UNIT 12

# Jobs

## Activity 1 (1' 25")

| | |
|---|---|
| accountant | journalist |
| architect | librarian |
| bank clerk | lorry driver |
| car mechanic | model |
| cashier | nurse |
| computer programmer | pilot |
| dentist | police officer |
| designer | receptionist |
| doctor | sales assistant |
| engineer | secretary |
| estate agent | social worker |
| hairdresser | university lecturer |

## Activity 2 (1' 52")

You will hear people describing some of the things they do at work. Listen and tick the activities they describe.

1   Well, when people come in to borrow some money from the bank, I have to talk to them and ask them a lot of questions, about who they are, where they work, how much money they have, and so on.

2   I meet the guests at the airport and drive them to their hotel.

3   I spend most of my day in front of the typewriter. We have so many letters to send out every day.

4   Well, my job is to find the right kind of house for people. They tell me the kind of house they want to buy and I try to find them something suitable which is for sale.

5   Well, the first thing I have to do every morning is to go round and give everyone their post.

6   Yes, people bring in their televisions when they break and I try to mend them.

7   As soon as each machine is made, my job is to make sure it works properly before we sell it. I have to look over each machine very carefully.

8   I wait for the doctor's patients to phone every morning and tell me when they want to come in for an appointment.

## Activity 3 (1' 30")

You will hear people talking about their occupations. Listen and number six of the occupations below from 1 - 6.

1   Yes, it's a wonderful job. I like teaching. I also like the long summer holidays. The students are very nice, too.
2   It's an interesting job, but I often have to work long hours at the hospital. Sometimes I start work at eleven in the morning and work through till ten in the evening.
3   It's a good job. People come from all over the world to stay at our hotel, because we're famous for our food.
4   I've always wanted to do this kind of work. I love cars and engines. Of course, it's quite dirty work, but the money's good.
5   It's all right. I like typing and the people in my office are very nice to work with.
6   I love my work. I'm able to wear all sorts of strange and beautiful costumes, and it's exciting to see photographs of myself in the theatrical magazines.

## Activity 4 (1' 32")

You will hear people talking about the jobs they used to have and the jobs they have now. Listen and tick their present job.

1   Yes, I really like my new job. I find it's more interesting being a nurse than a social worker.
2   The job at the library was too boring. Now I work in a shop and I meet lots of interesting people.
3   Well, my salary was higher when I was a driver, but I do get a lot of money in tips.
4   I love my job. When I was at the hospital I had to work every night. Now I just work from nine till five.
5   Well, I don't work with computers any more in my new job. I work with money. That's much more interesting.
6   The thing I didn't like about being a driver was the long trips away from home. The garage where I'm working now is just five minutes away.
7   It's different working in an office from working at a college. But I like it. I don't have to correct students' homework.

## Activity 5 (1' 08")

You will hear Ms Patel telling her secretary what she wants her to do today. Listen and number five of the activities below from 1 - 5 in the order she talks about them.

Now, first of all, could you call up Mr Stevens? I'd like to meet him on Friday at 10 a.m. Then I'll need the sales report. Could you finish typing it this morning, please? Don't forget to go to the post office after lunch. I need to send a package to Switzerland. Then perhaps you could call British Airways and try to get me on a flight to Paris on the 16th. See if you can get me a hotel too, will you?

Oh, and I won't be able to meet Ms Cairns this afternoon. I've got to go to the airport. Could you call her and tell her? Perhaps she can meet me on Thursday.

## Activity 6 (45")

Jane is staring a new job in an office. Helen is showing her where things are in the stationery cupboard. Listen and number the correct place in the picture.

The letter paper is here on the second shelf, on the left-hand side and the envelopes are on the top shelf, on the right. You'll find pens next to the letter paper and notebooks on the top shelf, on the left hand side. On the bottom shelf there are elastic bands and sellotape. The elastic bands are on the right and the sellotape is on the left.

## Activity 7 (1' 55")

Listen to people asking where places are in an office block. Each person is at X. Number the correct places.

1   A   Where's the coffee bar, please?
    B   It's on the next floor up, at the end of the corridor on the right.

2   A   I'm looking for the accounts department.
    B   It's the last door on the right.

3   A   Where's the manager's office, please?
    B   It's the first door on the left.

4   A   Where's the toilet, please?
    B   It's on the next floor up, the last door on the left, opposite the coffee bar.

5   A   Am I on the right floor for Mr Smith's office?
    B   No, you'll have to go upstairs. It's the office at the top of the stairs, on the left.

6   A   Where's the stationery store?
    B   There's one upstairs, next to Mr Smith's office.

7   A   Which is Ms Randall's office?
    B   It's the second door on the right.

8   A   Where's the photocopier, please?
    B   At the end of the corridor, on the left.

9   A   Where's the post room, please?
    B   Just here on the right.

# Leaving messages

## Activity 1 (2')

Listen to people ringing an office to ask to speak to someone. The person is not in. Tick what the callers will do.

1   A   Could I speak to Miss Cole, please?
    B   She's on another line at the moment. Would you like to wait?
    A   All right.

2  A  Mr Sampson, please.
   B  I'm afraid he's at a meeting right now. Would you like to leave a message?
   A  Well, is Mr Day there?
   B  Yes, just a moment.

3  A  May I speak to Miss Hennings?
   B  I'm afraid she's not in. Would you like to leave a message?
   A  Well, actually, I wanted to meet her tomorrow at ten. Is she free?
   B  Yes, she is. Your name, please?

4  A  Is Mr Platt in, please?
   B  He's busy right now. Would you like to leave a message?
   A  It's all right. I'll call back this afternoon.

5  A  Mrs Gordon, please.
   B  I'm sorry, she's not here today.
   A  Oh. Then could I speak to Mr Harper, please?
   B  Yes, just a moment.

6  A  I'd like to speak to Mrs Wilson, please.
   B  She's at a conference at the moment I'm afraid.
   A  Oh. Could you ask her to call Ted Collins on 467 3445?
   B  Yes, all right.

# Job interviews

## Activity 1 (1' 51")

Listen to four people being interviewed for jobs. Tick the correct information below.

1  A  And did you go to college?
   B  No, just secondary school.
   A  I see. Now let me tell you a little about the job. We make television sets here and also car radios.
   B  That sounds interesting.
   A  Have you ever worked in a factory?
   B  No, I haven't.

2  A  So you went to college in Ireland, did you?
   B  That's right.
   A  Now, most of our guests come from Europe. Do you speak any foreign languages?
   B  I speak a little French and Spanish.
   A  Very good. Have you worked in a hotel before?
   B  I worked in a small hotel for three months once in the summer.

3  A  Could you tell me about your education?
   B  I left school last month.
   A  I see. Now in this shop we sell mostly to tourists. Do you like meeting people?
   B  Yes, I do.
   A  Good. Have you had any experience working in a shop?
   B  No, I haven't.

4  A  And when did you leave college?
   B  I graduated from Ealing Technical College in 1980.
   A  I see. You'll be working in the library; the doctors use the library a lot and some of the nurses do, too.
   B  Fine.
   A  Now, you say you worked in a hospital library in India?
   B  Yes, for five years.

## Activity 2 (1' 06")

You will hear questions from a job interview. Listen and choose the best answer to each question.

1  What did you do before you came to Europe?
2  Have you got a driving licence?
3  How many languages can you speak?
4  How well do you type?
5  Where did you go to college?
6  How many years were you at college?
7  How long were you in your last job?
8  What was your salary in your last job?

# UNIT 13

# Leisure activities

## Activity 2 (1' 45")

You will hear short telephone conversations. What was each person doing when the phone rang? Number six of the pictures below from 1 - 6.

1  A  Hello Sandy. It's Karen here.
   B  Oh, hello.
   A  What are you doing?
   B  I'm still studying for next week's exam. I think it's going to be a difficult one.

2  A  Hello Betty. Everything nearly ready for the party?
   B  Not quite. I've still got some cakes to make and I haven't started on the vegetables yet.

3  A  Is that you John? This is Ted.
   B  Oh hello. Listen, can I call you back later? I want to watch the last few minutes of the game. Aren't you watching it?

4  A  Hi, Mark. How's everything?
   B  I'm a bit busy right now. We've got guests coming for the weekend and the house is so untidy. I hate housework!

5  A  Oh, hello Fran. Are you busy at the moment?
   B  Not really. I was just reading about that awful fire last night at the Palace Hotel.
   A  Oh yes, that was pretty bad.

6  A  Jane, this is Margaret. Are you busy?
   B  Well yes. Actually I'm just painting the ceiling.

## Activity 3 (2' 05")

You will hear people talking about the things they like and don't like doing in their spare time. Listen and tick how much they like each activity.

1  Well, I don't mind playing cards sometimes. But I prefer playing snooker myself. It's a little more exciting.
2  Everybody else in my family really loves sports. My brother's a very good tennis player and my sister's an excellent swimmer. I just find all sports boring and a waste of time.
3  I enjoy them from to time but not too often. I don't like meeting people all that much. When I know everybody there, then I enjoy it.
4  I wish I could eat out every night. It's so nice not to have to cook and wash up.
5  Yes, Tim and I go dancing about twice a week, and more often sometimes. It's a great way to relax and meet people.
6  I used to watch TV every night. Last year the programmes were really good. But I don't like this year's programmes as much. There are only a few I really like watching.
7  Oh yes, I have the radio on all the time. Mostly I prefer pop music but sometimes I also listen to classical music or jazz.
8  I never use my kitchen except to make coffee. It's so much easier to eat out. Of course, it costs more but it's much more fun.

## Activity 4 (1' 24")

Listen to people getting ready to do something. Tick what you think they're going to do.

1  Well, it's a nice day and it's not very windy. I don't think the water will be too rough. Don't forget to bring the towels, will you?
2  Hurry up, now. I asked for a table for eight o' clock, so we don't want to be late.
3  Have you got the tickets? Now what time does it start? Is it eight o' clock?
4  There are three new players in our team this week. I hope they're good.
5  Well, there's a film on Central at 7.30. It's got Madonna in it. I hear it's very good.
6  Could you get the table ready? I want to tidy the bathroom before they get here.
7  I'll bring the ketchup. Have you got the meat and the potatoes?

## Activity 5 (1' 40")

You will hear people talking about things they've done. Listen and tick how much they enjoyed them.

1  A  What did you think of the film?

B  Well, the music was good and the colour was beautiful, but the story was pretty boring. I fell asleep twice!
2  A  How was the party?
   B  Huh. Do you like loud music, lots of cigarette smoke, a small crowded room, and not enough food?

3  A  Did you enjoy the concert?
   B  It was the best concert I've been to in years. It was great music and it was beautifully played.

4  A  What did you think of the lecture?
   B  She had some interesting things to say at first, then it got very difficult to understand.

5  A  How was the restaurant?
   B  Well, my steak was overcooked, and the waitress was quite rude. I don't think I'll go there again.

6  A  What was Bill and Vicki's party like?
   B  So many interesting people and wonderful food.

7  A  Thanks for returning the book. How did you like it?
   B  I couldn't put it down. She writes so well and the story's very exciting.

# Invitations and arrangements

## Activity 1 (1' 25")

You will hear people inviting a friend to go somewhere with them. Listen and tick whether they said 'yes' or 'no'.

1  A  How about going to a disco tonight?
   B  I'd love to, but I've got to do some homework.

2  A  Would you like to see a film at the weekend?
   B  I'd love to. I haven't seen one for ages.

3  A  Any plans for tomorrow night? There's an interesting lecture at the museum.
   B  Not tomorrow. There's something I've got to do.

4  A  How about having dinner together over the weekend?
   B  Oh, that would be nice.

5  A  Do you want to play tennis on Sunday afternoon?
   B  Oh, I've got friends coming round on Sunday, I'm afraid.

6  A  Like to have a drink after work?
   B  I've got to work late today. Some other time, maybe.

7  A  Why don't we go to the beach this Saturday?
   B  Great. What time do you want to meet?

## Activity 2 (1' 37")

Listen to people arranging to do something. What are they going to do? Write down the day they will meet and the time.

1  A  How about going to see Rocky 6 on Saturday?
   B  Oh, I've already seen it.
   A  Would you like to go dancing, then?
   B  I'd love to.
   A  Shall we meet around nine o' clock at Spat's?
   B  OK. See you on Saturday at nine.

2  A  Why don't we eat in town this weekend?
   B  That'd be nice.
   A  Do you like Italian food?
   B  Yes, I love it.
   A  Is Sunday night any good for you?
   B  I'd prefer Saturday.
   A  Right. Let's meet here at 7.30.
   B  Fine.

3  A  It's Josie's birthday on Friday. Shall we go over to her place? She's invited a lot of people.
   B  Yes, let's. What time on Friday?
   A  She asked us to come at about seven.

4  A  Let's go to the park on Sunday afternoon.
   B  Good idea.
   A  We could take some sandwiches and have lunch by the river.
   B  Yes, and I can cook some chicken. What time do you want to go?
   A  Let's leave around eleven o' clock.

## Activity 3 (55")

Choose the best response to the questions you hear.

1  Doing anything this weekend?
2  Do you like Mexican food?
3  What did you think of the lecture?
4  Do you play much sport?
5  How about going to a film tonight?
6  Do you like playing cards?
7  How was your weekend?
8  Did you enjoy the party?

# UNIT 14

# Instructions

## Activity 2 (1' 28")

Listen to people describing how to use different pieces of equipment. Number the things they talk about in the correct order, from 1 - 4.

1  Well, you go into the booth and you'll see the machine on the wall. Put in two 50p coins. Press the button at the side. Now sit on the chair and look at the red light.

2  First you have to choose how many hours you want to park. Now put your money in at the top and the ticket comes out here at the bottom.

3  Right. You start by putting your money in here. Then choose how you want your coffee - black, with milk, with sugar. Now press the button marked start. You take your coffee out here.

4  First, choose the size you want. Next, choose the number of copies you need. Now put your document down flat on top of the glass here. Then close the lid and press the start button.

## Activity 3 (1' 05")

You will hear a recipe for chicken cooked with aubergine, garlic, sauce and herbs. Listen to the instructions and number eight of the sentences from 1 - 8.
It's quite simple really. First cut up the garlic into very small pieces. Next cut up the chicken into very thin slices. After that cut up the aubergine, also into thin slices. Now fry the garlic until itturns light brown. Then add the chicken and the aubergine to the frying pan and stir it in. Then add the sauce and the herbs. Lastly, add two cups of water. Now leave it to cook for ten minutes.

## Activity 4 (1' 20")

You will hear a sales assistant telling a customer how to look after some of the things below. Number six of them from 1 - 6 in the order in which you hear them.

1  Well, you can clean it with a vacuum cleaner, of course. Or you can wash it by hand, too, if you want to. You can also take it to a dry cleaner.
2  Don't wash them in the washing machine. It's better to take them to a dry cleaner to be cleaned.
3  You can wash him with shampoo in the bath once a week. He will like it and it'll keep him nice and clean.
4  Keep it in a cool place. Don't put it near a window or the sun will make the water too hot.
5  Keep the needle clean at all times or it'll damage your records. You can use a clean soft cloth to clean your records.
6  Polish it once a week with a good polish. Don't put anything hot on it and don't spill water or liquids on it.

## Activity 5 (1' 30")

Listen to a sales assistant telling someone how to clean and look after different things. Tick the advice the sales assistant gives.

1  You should wash these by hand. It's better not to wash them in the washing machine.
2  These should be washed in the washing machine to get them really clean.
3  Don't use hot water to wash these. Use warm water only.
4  It's best to wash these by hand in warm water. Don't dry clean them or they may lose their colour.

5  You can't iron this cloth. Just hang it up to dry.
6  You can use a fine oil to clean this table. Don't use soap and water on it at any time.
7  Just put these in the washing machine when they're dirty.
8  The dishwasher won't clean these very well, so you'll have to wash them by hand.

## Activity 6 (1' 43")

Listen to these customers saying what they need done. Tick what they want.

1  Just a little off the top and sides, please. Not too short.

2  A  Would you like me to shampoo it first?
   B  It's all right, thanks. I'll do it myself at home.

3  Now when you've washed this, could you mend this little hole at the back, please?

4  A  Shall I fill the tank, sir?
   B  Yes, please.

5  A  I wonder if you can fix this leg, please. It's quite loose.
   B  And then you want it painted dark brown?
   A  No, light brown, please.

6  A  Now, would you like a polish as well as a check-up?
   B  Yes, that's a good idea.

7  A  Do you want us to paint it when we finish the repairs?
   B  It's all right. I'll paint it myself.

8  A  Now, you want it cleaned. And would you like a new strap?
   B  No, I think the strap's all right, thanks.

9  A  So you want these heeled. And would you like new soles as well?
   B  Um, yes please.

## Activity 7 (1' 14")

Mrs Potter is asking her children to do things. She wants them to do some things now and some things later. Tick what she wants them to do first.

1  You can make the beds after you finish ironing the clothes.
2  Let's wash the dishes and then we can tidy the living room.
3  I don't think the plants need watering right away but the cooker really does need cleaning.
4  Before you cut up the vegetables, could you cut up the meat?
5  Clean the windows before you do the dishes.
6  You'd better polish the table. We can do the vacuuming later.
7  After you tidy the bedrooms, I'd like you to clean the bathroom.

## Activity 8 (1' 18")

Your flatmate Elaine likes moving things around in your flat. Listen to her deciding what to change. Draw a line from each item to its new position. She makes six changes.

1  You know, the bookcase doesn't look very nice near the window. Why don't we bring it over here by the door?
2  I think that new painting will look better in the dining room than in the living room. Let's move it.
3  I think we'll bring the coffee table out of the study and put it back here in the living room.
4  Why don't we move that rug back to the smaller bedroom? It doesn't look right in the living room.
5  That vase would look nice in the dining room. I don't really like it in my bedroom.
6  Shall I take the typewriter back to the study? I've finished with it.

# UNIT 15

# Airports

## Activity 2 (1' 14")

You will hear sentences containing some of the places below. Number the places you hear from 1 - 7.

1  Please take this to immigration.
2  You'll find a telephone booth at the end of the lounge.
3  The restaurant is on the next floor.
4  You should wait by the departure gate.
5  Please ask at the information desk.
6  I'll meet you in the departure lounge.
7  There's a post office next to the bank.

## Activity 3 (1' 44")

Listen to airport announcements for the people below. Match each name with the correct announcement.

1  Calling Fiona Johnson. Fiona Johnson. Please go to the meeting point.
2  Yau Chit Man. Yau Chit Man. Please meet your party at the Cathay Pacific check-in.
3  Mr Hisashi Uematsu. Mr Hisashi Uematsu. Please report immediately to the Japan Airlines ticket counter.
4  Calling Linda Kennedy. Linda Kennedy. Please come to the Singapore Airlines desk.
5  Mr Henri Bourassa. Mr Henri Bourassa. Please go to the Air France desk for a message.
6  Jean Halpern. Calling Ms Jean Halpern. Please go at once to the information desk.

## Activity 4 (3' 30")

Listen to these airport announcements and complete the missing information about each flight.

1   Announcing the departure of flight BA 445 to Athens at 20.35, gate number 16. BA 445 at 20.35, gate number 16.
2   Announcing the departure of flight BA 116 to Mexico City leaving at 16.45 from gate number 13. Flight BA116 at 16.45 from gate number 13. This flight is now boarding.
3   British Airways announce the departure of flight BA 360 to Boston, leaving at 15.25 from gate 7. Last call for flight BA 360 to Boston, leaving at 15.25 from gate 7.
4   Announcing the departure of TWA flight 44 to Los Angeles, departing at 6.05, gate number 12. TWA flight 44 at 6.05, gate number 12.
5   Japan Airlines announce the departure of flight 176 to Tokyo at 5.45, boarding at gate 17. Flight JAL 176 at 5.45, gate 17.
6   World Airlines announce the departure of flight 375 to San Francisco, boarding at gate 3 at 5.10. Flight WA 375 leaving at 5.10 from gate number 3.
7   Air France announce the departure of flight AF 86 for Paris, leaving at 11.15 from gate 15. Flight AF 86 leaving at 11.15 from gate 15.

## Activity 5 (2' 16")

The people below have just arrived at the airport. They want different kinds of hotel accommodation. They each dial a hotel and receive a recorded message. Listen to the message and tick what you think each caller will do next.

1   Thank you for calling the Plaza Hotel. The Plaza Hotel offers first-class accommodation with rooms starting at £55 a night . . .
2   This is the Orchard Hotel. The Orchard Hotel offers you comfortable and convenient accommodation in the heart of the business district and only minutes away from the central shops and offices. Rooms at the Orchard Hotel . . .
3   Welcome to the Seaview Hotel. With a beautiful view of the sea from all rooms and just a short walk to the beach, the Seaview offers reasonably-priced family accommodation. To make a reservation . . .
4   This is the Shangri-la Hotel. The hotel is situated in the centre of the city. The Shangri-la Hotel has rooms priced from £50 to £100 a night . . .
5   Thank you for calling the Regent Hotel. The Regent is located in the centre of the city, near the British Museum, and is about one hour by bus from the airport. Prices start at . . .
6   Welcome to the Miranda Hotel. The Miranda offers clean and comfortable accommodation for the business traveller, with prices starting at £45 a night. All rooms are single rooms at the Miranda . . .

## Activity 6 (1' 56")

You will hear people who have just arrived at an airport phoning friends. Their friends are out. They leave a message on their friend's answering machine. Tick the messages they leave.

1   Hello, Jean. This is Annette. I'm at the airport. Our plane's stopped for an hour and we leave shortly for New York. How is everyone? Sorry we didn't manage to have a chat.
2   Hello. This is David. I've just arrived at the airport. I'm having trouble finding a hotel. Can I stay with you for a few days? I'll call you back in an hour.
3   Good afternoon. This is Don Wilson. I've just arrived and I'll be booking into the Plaza Hotel. Can you call me there this evening?
4   Hello. This is Brenda. I'm here for a few days to attend a conference. I hope we can get together soon. I'm staying at the Convention Hotel.
5   Hello. This is Nigel. I've just got here. I'll be busy for the next couple of days, but can we meet on Saturday or Sunday? I'll call you tonight.
6   This is Janet Simpson. I've just arrived. Are you free to have dinner with me tonight? I'd like to take you out to a nice restaurant.

# Immigration

## Activity 1 (1' 18")

You will hear questions asked by a customs or immigration officer at the airport. Tick the best answer to each question.

1   How long are you going to be here?
2   What's the purpose of your visit?
3   How much money did you bring with you?
4   Where will you be staying?
5   What flight did you arrive on?
6   Is anyone travelling with you?
7   May I see your passport?
8   Which one is your bag?

# UNIT 1

## Numbers

### Activity 2

| | | | | | |
|---|---|---|---|---|---|
| 1 | 22 | 4 | 1010 | 7 | 1559 |
| 2 | 190 | 5 | 70 | | |
| 3 | 13 | 6 | 151 | | |

### Activity 3

| | | | | |
|---|---|---|---|---|
| 7th prize | 115 | 3rd prize | 59 |
| 6th prize | 1770 | 2nd prize | 1990 |
| 5th prize | 19 | 1st prize | 40 |
| 4th prize | 309 | | |

## Telephone Numbers

### Activity 2

| | | | | | |
|---|---|---|---|---|---|
| 1 | 313597 | 4 | 0519 23092 | 7 | 068 91 789 |
| 2 | 743678 | 5 | 0457 64332 | 8 | 339279 |
| 3 | 01 808 7688 | 6 | 041 904 5308 | 9 | 0425 5781 |

### Activity 4

| | | | |
|---|---|---|---|
| 1 | Oxford 64711 | 4 | 01 388 0542 |
| 2 | 021 930 2738 | 5 | Bristol 88070 |
| 3 | 061 439 4576 | 6 | 031 897 4567 |

### Activity 5

| | | | | | |
|---|---|---|---|---|---|
| 1 | wrong | 3 | wrong | 5 | wrong |
| 2 | right | 4 | wrong | 6 | right |

## Addresses

### Activity 1

| | | | |
|---|---|---|---|
| 1 | 89 Mount Street | 4 | 2 Portman Street W1 |
| 2 | 103 Waterloo Road | 5 | 193 Picadilly |
| 3 | 623 Holloway Road | 6 | 256 Grays Inn Road |

### Activity 2

| | | | | | |
|---|---|---|---|---|---|
| 1 | 313 | 3 | 59 | 5 | 206/15 |
| 2 | 615/19 | 4 | 109 | | |

# UNIT 2

## Names

### Activity 2

| | | | |
|---|---|---|---|
| 1 | Short | 5 | Richmond |
| 2 | Thomas | 6 | Simpson |
| 3 | Johnson | 7 | Jones |
| 4 | Gray | 8 | Smith |

### Activity 3

1 Eddie
2 Michael
3 Steffi
4 Humphrey
5 Margaret
6 Madonna

### Activity 5

| | | | |
|---|---|---|---|
| 1 | Tosh Asada | 5 | Gerald Kirkby |
| 2 | Monika Manning | 6 | Francine La Tuille |
| 3 | Karl Gass | 7 | Richard Forsythe |
| 4 | Sophie Jacobs | 8 | Martha Pennington |

### Activity 6

| | | | |
|---|---|---|---|
| 1 | wrong Jessie Bowman | 5 | right |
| 2 | wrong Trisha Everett | 6 | right |
| 3 | right | 7 | wrong Robert Cohen |
| 4 | wrong Carla Mestanza | 8 | wrong Bradley Metcalfe |

### Activity 7

| | | | |
|---|---|---|---|
| 1 | Dr P M Agrabanti | 5 | Dr J D Blackburn |
| 2 | Ms K Foster | 6 | Miss C C Chun |
| 3 | Mr M P Corpuz | 7 | Mr D V Lange |
| 4 | Miss K Kato | 8 | Mrs B Corrigan |

## Meeting people

### Activity 1

| | | | |
|---|---|---|---|
| 1 | Fine, thanks. | 6 | Richard. Richard Deakin. |
| 2 | Yes, lovely. | 7 | Yes, you too. |
| 3 | Great. And yours? | 8 | How do you do? |
| 4 | Oh, O.K. thanks. | 9 | Not too bad. |
| 5 | Mine's Jenny. Hello. | 10 | Yeah, O.K. |
| | | 11 | You too. |

### Activity 2

| | | | |
|---|---|---|---|
| 1 | That's right. | 4 | How do you do? |
| 2 | Fine, thanks. | 5 | Fine, thanks. |
| 3 | Nice to meet you, too. | 6 | Nice to meet you. |

## Places

### Activity 1

| | | | |
|---|---|---|---|
| 1 | Berkshire | 5 | Lancashire |
| 2 | Cornwall | 6 | Tayside |
| 3 | Durham | 7 | Strathclyde |
| 4 | Gwent | 8 | West Glamorgan |

### Activity 2

| | | | |
|---|---|---|---|
| 1 | Colorado | 5 | Pennsylvania |
| 2 | Indiana | 6 | Arizona |
| 3 | Illinois | 7 | Montana |
| 4 | Alabama | 8 | Oregon |

### Activity 3

| | | | |
|---|---|---|---|
| 1 | Manchester | 5 | Barcelona |
| 2 | Paris | 6 | France |
| 3 | Hong Kong | 7 | Ecuador |
| 4 | St Louis | 8 | Oxford |

### Activity 4

| | | | |
|---|---|---|---|
| Asia - 3 | | South America - 1 | |
| Africa - 2 | | Middle East - 1 | |
| Europe - 2 | | Pacific - 1 | |

## UNIT 3

# Times

### Activity 3

| | | | |
|---|---|---|---|
| 1 | 7.45 | 5 | 13.45 |
| 2 | 15.20 | 6 | 11.15 |
| 3 | 20.30 | 7 | 8.05 |
| 4 | 16.40 | 8 | 18.25 |

### Activity 4

| | | | |
|---|---|---|---|
| Mr Day | 11.00 | Mrs Ginatti | 11.30 |
| Ms Lewis | 10.15 | Mr Frank | 10.45 |
| Mr Grant | 11.00 | Ms Taylor | 10.40 |

### Activity 5

| | | | |
|---|---|---|---|
| Bolivia | 10 a.m. | Burma | 11.30 p.m. |
| Haiti | 12 p.m. | Taiwan | 6.30 p.m. |
| Finland | 8.30 a.m. | Fiji | 7 p.m. |
| Argentina | 10.15 a.m. | Germany | 10.15 a.m. |

# Dates

### Activity 2

1 Charles Dickens: 1812 - 1870
2 D H Lawrence: 1885 - 1930
3 Jane Austen: 1775 - 1817
4 Ernest Hemingway: 1899 - 1961
5 Emily Dickinson: 1830 - 1886
6 Oscar Wilde: 1854 - 1900

### Activity 4

| | | | |
|---|---|---|---|
| 1 | 6/6/39 | 4 | 16/2/29 |
| 2 | 6/7/65 | 5 | 2/1/44 |
| 3 | 21/4/56 | 6 | 15/11/71 |

### Activity 5

| | | | |
|---|---|---|---|
| 1 | 4/20 | 4 | 10/20 |
| 2 | 10/22 | 5 | 6/25 |
| 3 | 5/19 | 6 | 1/20 |

### Activity 6

| | | | |
|---|---|---|---|
| 1 | 6 ½ weeks | 5 | 26 years |
| 2 | 16 years | 6 | 4 ½ weeks |
| 3 | 3 ½ months | 7 | 5 years |
| 4 | 9 months | 8 | 5 weeks |

## UNIT 4

# Food

### Activity 1

| meat | fish | vegetables |
|---|---|---|
| beef<br>chicken<br>turkey<br>lamb | tuna<br>sole<br>salmon<br>lobster | cucumber<br>onion<br>cabbage<br>mushroom<br>broccoli<br>corn<br>cauliflower |

| fruit | cereals |
|---|---|
| mango<br>pineapple<br>apple<br>orange<br>grapefruit<br>pear | wheat<br>rice |

### Activity 2

| | | | |
|---|---|---|---|
| 1 | the | 5 | a |
| 2 | a | 6 | the |
| 3 | the | 7 | a |
| 4 | a | | |

### Activity 3

broccoli/rice/onions/bread/lamb

# Recipes

### Activity 1

1 800g beef
250g onions
3 tbsp tomato puree
1 ½ tbsp curry powder
½ tsp salt
¼ tsp pepper

2   6 eggs
    200g sliced onions
    250g mushrooms
    ½ l cream
    ½ tsp salt
    ½ tsp pepper
    175g cheese

3   1 kg chicken
    250g onions
    150g bacon
    ¼ l red wine
    75g flour

# In a restaurant

## Activity 1

| 1 | chicken | 2 | beef/rare | 3 | fish |
|---|---------|---|-----------|---|------|
|   | potatoes |  | rice      |   | rice |
|   | fruit juice |  | vegetables |  | vegetables |
|   |          |   | coffee    |   |      |

## Activity 2

1   Yes, they liked it a lot.
2   Yes, they quite liked it.
3   No, they didn't like it at all.
4   No, they didn't like it at all.
5   Yes, they liked it a lot.
6   Yes, they quite liked it.

## Activity 3

1   not hot enough         5   undercooked
2   overcooked             6   too spicy
3   not salty enough       7   too much sugar
4   too tough

## Activity 4

1   Yes, it's fine.        5   Just a little.
2   Fine, thanks.          6   Yes, it's great.
3   No, thanks.            7   Not just now.
4   No, thanks.

# UNIT 5

# Furniture and rooms

## Activity 1

| *the kitchen* | *the living room* | *the bathroom* |
|---------------|-------------------|----------------|
| a cooker | a sofa | a wash basin |
| a fridge | a fireplace | a shower |
| a sink | a television | *a bedroom* |
| a washing | a stereo system | a wardrobe |
| machine | a reading lamp | a chest of drawers |
|  | a bookcase | (a reading lamp) |
|  |  | (a bookcase) |

## Activity 2

1   a <u>coo</u>ker
2   a <u>show</u>er
3   a <u>fire</u>place
4   a <u>wash</u>ing ma<u>chine</u>
5   a <u>ward</u>robe
6   a <u>ste</u>reo <u>sy</u>stem
7   a <u>book</u>case
8   a <u>te</u>levision

## Activity 3

1 a    2 b    3 b    4 b    5 a

## Activity 4

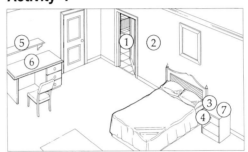

## Activity 5

1 a    5 a
2 b    6 b
3 b    7 b
4 a    8 a

# At home

## Activity 1

| Kathy | - | in the garage |
|-------|---|---------------|
| Bill | - | in the bedroom |
| Susan | - | in the bathroom |
| Terry | - | he has gone out |
| Mr Lee | - | in the kitchen |
| Helen | - | in the living room |

## Activity 2

*Roy*                        *Sylvia*
clean the bathroom           take out the rubbish
go shopping                  vacuum the carpet
clean the car                clean the windows
put away the groceries

*leave till later*
clean the fridge
iron the sheets

### Activity 3

1 Could you turn on the TV?
2 Could you get me something to eat?
3 Could you close the window?
4 Could you turn on the lamp?
5 Could you turn up the heating?

# UNIT 6

# Prices

### Activity 2

| | | |
|---|---|---|
| 1 £56.50 | 4 £1,067.00 | 7 £550.00 |
| 2 £11.17 | 5 £109.45 | 8 £15,670.00 |
| 3 £69.09 | 6 £198,000 | 9 £125,900 |
| | | 10 £1,350,000 |

### Activity 3

1 x    2 x    3 x    4 x

### Activity 4

| | | | |
|---|---|---|---|
| watch | $140 | = | £10 |
| calculator | $35 | = | £2.50 |
| cassette recorder | $11,360 | = | £50 |
| necklace | $91 | = | £25 |

### Activity 5

| | | | | |
|---|---|---|---|---|
| 1 | 1 London | 4 | 1 | San Francisco |
| | 2 Paris | | 2 | Chicago |
| | 3 Madrid | | 3 | Phoenix |
| 2 | 1 Tokyo | 5 | 1 | Los Angeles |
| | 2 New York | | 2 | Mexico City |
| | 3 London | | 3 | Hong Kong |
| 3 | 1 Tokyo | 6 | 1 | Jakarta |
| | 2 Honolulu | | 2 | Washington |
| | 3 Singapore | | 3 | Rio |

# Paying

### Activity 1

1 personal cheque
2 Barclaycard
3 cash
4 Access

### Activity 2

1 £50 x 7

2 £20 x 10
£50 x 3
£10 x 15

3 £50 x 20
£20 x 25

4 £20 x 5
£10 x 5

### Activity 3

| | | | |
|---|---|---|---|
| 1 | will buy something else | 4 | will buy |
| 2 | will buy | 5 | won't buy anything |
| 3 | won't buy anything | 6 | will buy something else |

### Activity 4

1 It's only £45.
2 No, this is the cheapest.
3 No, £1550.
4 Not more than £50.
5 The ring's cheaper.
6 £2.50 is enough.
7 Oh, did you?
8 Oh, I'm sorry. Let me check it again.

# UNIT 7

# Health

### Activity 1

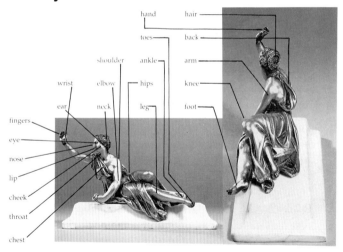

### Activity 2

| | | | |
|---|---|---|---|
| 1 | nose | 5 | throat |
| 2 | neck | 6 | wrist |
| 3 | hips | 7 | ears |
| 4 | hair | 8 | leg |

## Activity 3

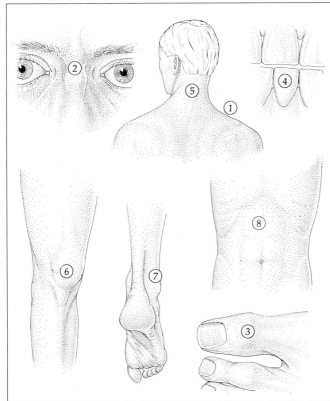

## Activity 4

1 He's got a cold.
2 She's got a headache.
3 She's got a stiff neck.
4 He's got a sore finger.
5 She's got toothache.
6 He's got a sore foot.
7 She's got a sore throat.
8 He's got earache.

## Activity 5

| 1 | 1 tsp | x2 | 5 | 2 tab | x2 |
| 2 | 2 tab | x3 | 6 | 3 tsp | x3 |
| 3 | 1 tab | x1 | 7 | 2 tab | x2 |
| 4 | 1 1/2 tsp | x6 | | | |

## Activity 6

| 1 | d | 5 | b |
| 2 | a | 6 | h |
| 3 | g | 7 | c |
| 4 | f | 8 | e |

## Activity 7

1 Oh, that's good.
2 Oh, that's too bad.
3 How did he do that?
4 Have you taken anything for it?
5 What's the matter?
6 Oh, good.
7 Why don't you take something for it?

# Exercise

## Activity 1

1 swims regularly
2 plays sports
3 walks
4 rides a bicycle
5 exercises regularly
6 runs
7 does daily exercise

# UNIT 8

# Describing objects

## Activity 1

digital ladies watch (5)
ladies black leather handbag with no strap (8)
man's sunglasses with metal frames (14)
small autofocus camera (3)
walkman with earphones (11)
short-sleeved child's jumper (2)
umbrella with curved handle (12)

## Activity 2

| 1 | radios | 3 | glass | 5 | watch | 7 | umbrella |
| 2 | shoe | 4 | brushes | 6 | suitcases | 8 | bottles |

## Activity 3

1 f (settee)      4 e (typewriter)   7 b (coffee table)
2 g (suitcase)   5 h (family car)
3 a (trainers)   6 c (rucksack)

## Activity 4

1 a    2 c    3 a    4 a    5 a    6 b    7 b

## Activity 5

1 too small
2 sleeves too short
3 doesn't keep correct time
4 no key for lock
5 earphones don't work
6 doesn't open properly
7 light isn't working

# Describing people

## Activity 1

## Activity 2

1  Paul  Tracy  Jenny  Kevin
2  Dad  Ellen  Karen  me  David
3  Dick  Susan  Margaret  Fred

## Activity 3

| | | | |
|---|---|---|---|
| 1 statement | | 5 question | |
| 2 question | | 6 statement | |
| 3 question | | 7 question | |
| 4 statement | | 8 statement | |

# UNIT 9

# Shops and shopping

## Activity 1

| | |
|---|---|
| bookshop | paperback |
| supermarket | weekend groceries, soft drinks |
| florist | plant |
| hardware store | frying pan, paint, ladder, garden tools |
| pet shop | dog food |
| furniture shop | coffee table |
| off-licence | wine |
| post office | stamps |
| bakery | bread and cakes |
| sports shop | tennis shoes |
| newsagent | photography magazine, newspaper |

## Activity 2

post office
furniture shop
pet shop
bakery

## Activity 3

| | bread | butter | milk | eggs |
|---|---|---|---|---|
| a lot | | ✓ | | ✓ |
| a little/a few | ✓ | | | |
| none at all | | | ✓ | |

| | sugar | vegetables | cooking oil | ketchup |
|---|---|---|---|---|
| a lot | | | ✓ | |
| a little/a few | ✓ | ✓ | | |
| none at all | | | | ✓ |

## Activity 4

1  Ace / easy to park
2  West's / bread is fresher
3  Betty's / staff friendly
4  Crest / more choice
5  University Bookshop / cheaper prices
6  Ellis's / the other shop is not open
7  Mullins / better vegetables

## Activity 5

| | |
|---|---|
| 1  television | 5  fridge |
| 2  bed | 6  camera |
| 3  car | 7  washing machine |
| 4  desk | 8  aquarium |

| item<br>age | 1 | 2 | 3 | 4 | 5 | 6 | 7 | 8 |
|---|---|---|---|---|---|---|---|---|
| less than 6 months old | | ✓ | | ✓ | | | | ✓ |
| less than a year old | ✓ | | | | | ✓ | ✓ | |
| over a year old | | | ✓ | | ✓ | | | |

## Activity 6

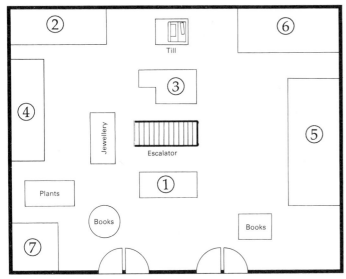

## Activity 7

| | | | |
|---|---|---|---|
| 1 | some perfume | 5 | the plate |
| 2 | a sweater | 6 | the necklace |
| 3 | the red blouse | 7 | the soap |
| 4 | the toy lorry | | |

# UNIT 10

## Going on holiday

### Activity 2

| | | | |
|---|---|---|---|
| 1 | go sightseeing | 4 | visit a museum or art gallery |
| 2 | go to a nightclub | 5 | go shopping |
| 3 | go to a restaurant | | |

### Activity 3

1  Japan, Hong Kong, Thailand
2  Holland, Spain, Greece
3  Los Angeles, San Francisco, Boston, New York
4  Paris, Brussels, Munich, Rome

### Activity 4

1  try the local food, go for a walk
2  go round the island by bus, take a boat trip, go skiing
3  go swimming, go shopping
4  visit museums, try Chinese food

### Activity 5

1  small suitcase, books, umbrella, coat
2  large suitcase, presents, personal stereo, swimsuit, medicine

## Activity 6

| | | | |
|---|---|---|---|
| 1 | liked everything | 5 | liked everything |
| 2 | liked some things | 6 | like some things |
| 3 | liked some things | 7 | liked everything |
| 4 | didn't like anything | | |

## Activity 7

| | | | |
|---|---|---|---|
| 1 | Very much, thanks. | 5 | Last week. |
| 2 | For about six weeks. | 6 | Not yet. |
| 3 | Until June. | 7 | About a month. |
| 4 | To Madrid. | 8 | It was great. |

# UNIT 11

## Transport

### Activity 1

| | | | | | |
|---|---|---|---|---|---|
| 1 | motor-bike | 5 | plane | 9 | moped |
| 2 | taxi | 6 | car | 10 | lorry |
| 3 | underground train | 7 | train | | |
| 4 | van | 8 | bicycle | | |

### Activity 2

| | | | |
|---|---|---|---|
| 1 | a blue moped | 5 | the green plane |
| 2 | a gold sports car | 6 | the fast train |
| 3 | a bright blue van | 7 | a dark brown Mini |
| 4 | a green bus | 8 | a light blue Toyota |

### Activity 3

| | | | |
|---|---|---|---|
| 1 | b | 4 | b |
| 2 | a | 5 | a |
| 3 | a | 6 | a |

### Activity 4

zoo: 17 or 24   20 mins
airport: 25   5 mins
museum: 44 or 50 every hour
university: 16 or 22   20mins
hospital: 65   45 mins
library: 13   15 mins

### Activity 5

| | | | |
|---|---|---|---|
| 1 | airport | 4 | theatre |
| 2 | restaurant | 5 | hospital |
| 3 | university | 6 | museum |

## Street directions

### Activity 1

1  Bank of Scotland
2  Everfresh Supermarket
3  Hong Kong Restaurant
4  Rose Hotel
5  Museum of Modern Art
6  Mediterranean Travel

**Activity 2** (numbers 1-6 on map)

**Activity 3** (letters A-F on map)

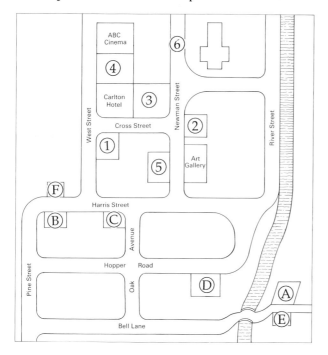

## UNIT 12

# Jobs

### Activity 1

| | |
|---|---|
| accountant | journalist |
| architect | librarian |
| bank clerk | lorry driver |
| car mechanic | model |
| cashier | nurse |
| computer programmer | pilot |
| dentist | police officer |
| designer | receptionist |
| doctor | sales assistant |
| engineer | secretary |
| estate agent | social worker |
| hairdresser | university lecturer |

### Activity 2

1 interview people
2 collect guests
3 type letters
4 sell houses
5 deliver post
6 repair TV sets
7 check machines
8 take telephone calls

### Activity 3

| | | | |
|---|---|---|---|
| 1 | university lecturer | 4 | mechanic |
| 2 | nurse | 5 | typist |
| 3 | hotel receptionist | 6 | actor |

### Activity 4

| | | | |
|---|---|---|---|
| 1 | nurse | 5 | bank clerk |
| 2 | shop assistant | 6 | mechanic |
| 3 | tour guide | 7 | office manager |
| 4 | receptionist | | |

### Activity 5

| | | | |
|---|---|---|---|
| 1 | arrange a meeting | 4 | make travel arrangements |
| 2 | type a report | 5 | cancel an appointment |
| 3 | post a package | | |

### Activity 6

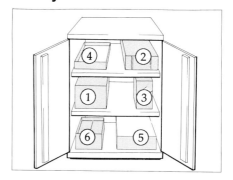

### Activity 7

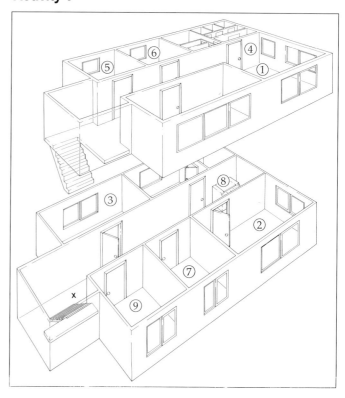

# Leaving messages

## Activity 1

| What caller will do | 1 | 2 | 3 | 4 | 5 | 6 |
|---|---|---|---|---|---|---|
| leave a message | | | | | | ✓ |
| make an appointment | | | ✓ | | | |
| call back later | | | | ✓ | | |
| wait | ✓ | | | | | |
| ask to speak to someone else | | ✓ | | | ✓ | |

*caller*

# Job interviews

## Activity 1

*interviewee*

| | | 1 | 2 | 3 | 4 |
|---|---|---|---|---|---|
| education | secondary school | ✓ | | ✓ | |
| | college / university | | ✓ | | ✓ |
| the job | office job | | | | |
| | factory job | ✓ | | | |
| | shop assistant | | | ✓ | |
| | hospital job | | | | ✓ |
| | hotel job | | ✓ | | |
| previous experience | a lot | | | | ✓ |
| | some | | ✓ | | |
| | none | ✓ | | ✓ | |

## Activity 2

1  I was a student.
2  Yes, I have.
3  Two.
4  Not very well.
5  In Edinburgh.
6  Three.
7  For two years.
8  £150 a week.

# Leisure activities

## Activity 2

1  g     4  f
2  e     5  a
3  h     6  c

## Activity 3

| | likes it a lot | likes it a little | doesn't like it at all |
|---|---|---|---|
| 1  playing cards | | ✓ | |
| 2  playing sports | | | ✓ |
| 3  going to parties | | ✓ | |
| 4  eating out | ✓ | | |
| 5  dancing | ✓ | | |
| 6  watching TV | | ✓ | |
| 7  listening to music | ✓ | | |
| 8  cooking | | | ✓ |

## Activity 4

1  go swimming
2  go to a restaurant
3  go to a concert
4  play basketball
5  watch TV
6  have friends round for dinner
7  go to a barbecue

## Activity 5

1  liked some things
2  didn't like anything
3  liked everything
4  liked some things
5  didn't like anything
6  liked everything
7  liked everything

# Invitations and arrangements

## Activity 1

1  No     5  No
2  Yes    6  No
3  No     7  Yes
4  Yes

## Activity 2

| 1 | disco | Sat | 9 o'clock |
|---|---|---|---|
| 2 | restaurant | Sat | 7.30 |
| 3 | party | Fri | 7 o'clock |
| 4 | picnic | Sun | 11 o'clock |

## Activity 3

1 Not really.
2 It's OK.
3 It was interesting.
4 Quite a bit.
5 Sorry, I'm not free.
6 Not really.
7 Fine, thanks.
8 Yes, it was great.

# UNIT 14

## Instructions

### Activity 2

1 b
2 c
3 a
4 d

### Activity 3

1 Cut up the garlic.
2 Cut up the chicken.
3 Cut up the aubergine.
4 Fry the garlic.
5 Fry the chicken and aubergine.
6 Add the sauce and herbs.
7 Add the water.
8 Cook it for ten minutes.

### Activity 4

1 c (rug)
2 f (curtains)
3 j (dog) or k(statue)
4 e (aquarium)
5 i (record player)
6 a (wooden table)

### Activity 5

1 handwash only
2 machine wash only
3 wash in warm water
4 do not dry clean
5 do not iron
6 clean with oil
7 wash in washing machine
8 wash by hand

### Activity 6

1 not cut much
2 cut only
3 washed and mended
4 full tank of petrol
5 repaired and painted
6 polished and checked
7 repaired
8 cleaned
9 heeled and soled

### Activity 7

1 iron the clothes
2 wash the dishes
3 clean the cooker
4 cut up the meat
5 clean the windows
6 polish the table
7 tidy the bedrooms

## Activity 8

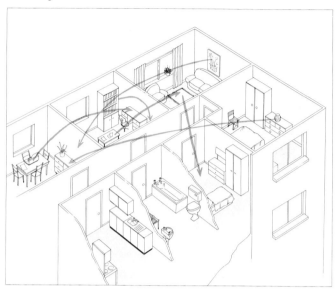

# UNIT 15

## Airports

### Activity 1

declare taxable goods — Customs
meet a friend who has just arrived — Arrivals
wait to board the plane — Departure Lounge
buy tax-free goods — Duty-free shop
get the seat number for a flight — Check- in
have a meal — Restaurant
have a sandwich — Snack bar
find out about sightseeing — Information desk
change some money — Bank
send a postcard — Post office

### Activity 2

1 immigration
2 telephone booth
3 restaurant
4 departure gate
5 information desk
6 departure lounge
7 post office

### Activity 3

1 go to the meeting point
2 go to Cathay Pacific check-in counter
3 go to Japan Airlines ticket counter
4 go to Singapore Airlines desk
5 message at Air France desk
6 report to information desk

## Activity 4

| 1 | BA445 | 20.35 | 16 |
|---|-------|-------|----|
| 2 | BA116 | 16.45 | 13 |
| 3 | BA360 | 15.25 | 7 |
| 4 | TWA44 | 6.05 | 12 |
| 5 | JAL176 | 5.45 | 17 |
| 6 | WA375 | 5.10 | 3 |
| 7 | AF86 | 11.15 | 15 |

## Activity 5

| 1 | try a different hotel | 4 | try a different hotel |
|---|-----------------------|---|-----------------------|
| 2 | make a reservation | 5 | make a reservation |
| 3 | make a reservation | 6 | try a different hotel |

## Activity 6

1  called to say 'Hello.'
2  wants a place to stay
3  call me at my hotel
4  in town for three or four days
5  wants to meet you at the weekend
6  invites you out to dinner

# Immigration

## Activity 1

| 1 | For a month. | 5 | SQ 250. |
|---|--------------|---|---------|
| 2 | To see friends. | 6 | No, I'm alone. |
| 3 | $1,500. | 7 | Here it is. |
| 4 | With friends. | 8 | The brown one. |